D0470626

First published in the United States of America in 2013 by
Quarry Books, a member of
Quayside Publishing Group
100 Cummings Center
Suite 406-L
Beverly, Massachusetts 01915-6101
Telephone: (978) 282-9590
Fax: (978) 283-2742
www.quarrybooks.com
Visit www.QuarrySPOON.com and help us celebrate food
and culture one spoonful at a time!

10 9 8 7 6 5 4 3 2 1

ISBN: 978-1-59253-870-6

Digital edition published in 2013
eISBN: 978-1-61058-889-8

Library of Congress Cataloging-in-Publication Data
Galchus, Rita.
 Homegrown sprouts : a fresh, healthy, and delicious step-
by-step guide to sprouting year round / Rita Galchus.
  p. cm.
 Includes index.
 ISBN 978-1-59253-870-6
 1. Sprouts. I. Title.
 SB324.53.G35 2013
 635'.34--dc23
                    2013024613

Design: Burge Agency
Photography: Thea Coughlin Photography
Author photo: Paul Galchus

Printed in China

HOMEGROWN
SPROUTS

RITA GALCHUS
"SPROUT LADY RITA"

A FRESH, HEALTHY, AND DELICIOUS STEP-BY-STEP
GUIDE TO SPROUTING YEAR ROUND

BEANS, GRAINS,
LEAFY GREENS,
WHEATGRASS,
AND MORE

CONTENTS

INTRODUCTION

I came to sprouting in April 1986 when my boyfriend, now my husband, took me on a date to an apartment in New York City, where we learned to sprout during a free class. I have been sprouting ever since. I remember so clearly today the taste of those homegrown sprouts: how natural and fresh their flavor was, how crunchy and crispy they felt on my tongue.

The demonstration showed the ease of the task—soak the seeds, rinse the seeds, eat the sprouts—so clearly that I knew I would be able to do it myself at home. We each purchased a starter kit and began to practice what we had learned right away. I took to sprouting quickly and had great success with those seeds. Even though I really had a black thumb when it came to caring for houseplants, my sprouts thrived.

Years passed, and my boyfriend and I married and had a son. In June 2000, I saw a classified ad: the sprouting business that held the free classes was for sale. I officially became Sprout Lady Rita on October 1, 2000.

At the time, I knew only one way to sprout two types of seed—alfalfa and mung beans in a small tray sprouter. But I was motivated to be successful at sprouting, so I experimented with the seeds that the business stocked and sold, and I read all I could. Little by little, seed by seed, sprout by sprout, I was able to learn which methods worked best for which seed. Yes, I failed at some, and there have been times that I have grown great and wonderful batches of mold and mildew without any recognizable sprout anywhere to be seen. Perseverance has allowed me to find the best and easiest methods to use to produce great sprouts time after time.

Many people come to sprouting and learn one technique with one or two seeds and one type of sprouter. I wrote this book to show that there are many different tools to use for sprouting, and that there are more seeds available than just alfalfa and mung bean. Sprouting at home can be a wonderful journey into tastes and textures. The seeds are beautiful to look at and offer unique aromas when inhaled. Additionally, sprouting can add great nutrition to our every meal.

Sprouters come in all ages and all sizes. They come to sprouting for a variety of reasons that usually include getting better nutrition from food. Sprouts can fit into any diet regardless of religious or political beliefs.

It does not take much time or effort to make a seed happy enough to sprout. We are all capable of being Mother Nature to these little guys so that they will grow into wonderful sprouts. The right amount of water at the right temperature and enough light when necessary is all that is needed to complete the cycle.

When he was a young boy, my son once said to me after eating some fenugreek sprouts, "Mom, this is what springtime tastes like." If you could assign a flavor to a season, I would match fresh sprouts to springtime, too. I invite you to take the journey with me!

—Sprout Lady Rita

CHAPTER 1:
THE BENEFITS OF SPROUTING

MANY PEOPLE ARE FAMILIAR WITH THE TWO MOST COMMON SPROUTS: ALFALFA AND MUNG BEAN. YOU MAY HAVE EATEN ALFALFA SPROUTS AT A RESTAURANT THAT FEATURES THEM ATOP A SALAD OR IN A CONTAINER AT THE SALAD BAR. MUNG BEANS ARE GROWN AS A COMPACT SHOOT, AND ARE FREQUENTLY USED IN CHINESE FOOD. BUT THERE IS A LARGER VARIETY OF SPROUTS AVAILABLE THAN JUST ALFALFA AND MUNG THAT CAN BE SPROUTED AT HOME. WITH A DIVERSITY OF WAYS TO SPROUT AND EAT THOSE TASTY LITTLE VEGETABLES, HOMEGROWN SPROUTS CAN BE A PART OF EVERY HOUSEHOLD KITCHEN.

WHY SPROUT?

Why choose to sprout at home? Here are some of the most popular reasons why homegrown sprouts are a wonderful choice.

HOMEGROWN TASTES BETTER

Homegrown sprouts taste better than commercially grown sprouts. Why? Because the sprouts you grow at home are fresh. They have not traveled from state to state or from a different country or continent. They have been raised right in your own kitchen. This is really the most local food you can get, and it's easy to do. The sprouts you buy at the store grow up in their little container somewhere along the way. Then they sit in the refrigerated section of the grocery store until someone buys them. Your homegrown sprouts are tended to in your kitchen by you.

SPROUTS ARE A HEALTHY OPTION

The first definition of the word diet is "what a person or animal eats or consumes." Any diet can include the eating of sprouts. There is no need to be a vegetarian, vegan, or raw foodist to enjoy sprouts. Sprouts can be served with any dish—cooked or raw, plant-based or not. It is an inclusive food, not exclusive. Eat a fresh, organic sprout salad with your steak, poultry, or fish. Sprouts can be eaten at all meals, even breakfast and snacks. The addition of sprouts to everyday eating and living can be very simple and life-changing results can occur— such as a reduced risk for chronic diseases and better colon health.

Sprouts are a great way to eat more vegetables. They are high in fiber, water, vitamins, and minerals. Shoots from leafy green sprouts like alfalfa, clover, sunflower, buckwheat, and speckled peas are high in chlorophyll and phytonutrients. The beans and legumes that you sprout are high in digestible protein. They have zero cholesterol, have very little fat, and are a low-sodium food. Sprouts are filled with the good types of carbohydrates, the ones you want to consume.

YOU CAN BOAST ABOUT YOUR SPROUTING ACCOMPLISHMENTS

You have bragging rights when you grow your own sprouts. Not everyone keeps to a sprouting schedule, although it is easy to do so. Once you start sprouting you can casually mention it to your friends, "Started my sprouts this morning before I came to work." "I am eating my homegrown sprouts for lunch today." "Would you like to eat some of my sprouts, the ones I grew at home, myself?"

VARIETY IS THE SPICE OF GOOD NUTRITION

You will be eating a wide variety of vegetables when you sprout. The key to getting the most nutrient value out of your food is to eat an assortment of fresh vegetables. Each vegetable contains different nutrients in different amounts. By eating a diverse selection of foods, you can get the nutrients you need, especially from a sprout you grew. Sprouted beans and legumes are high in protein. Leafy green sprouts can give us chlorophyll and vitamins. Adding fiber from sprouts to any diet is helpful, and a tasty way to get these nutrients.

SPROUTERS LOVE COMPANY

You can make a community of sprouters. It may not seem like there are many of us around, but once you start talking about your sprouting experience, you may find that there are others near you who do sprout or once sprouted or are thinking about starting sprouting.

Bring sprouts to a meeting or gathering that you attend instead of cookies from the convenience store. You might be surprised that at the end of the time spent together with other folks, your sprouts are gone.

SPROUTING MEANS TAKING CARE OF YOUR FAMILY

Sprouting will make you a better caretaker. You introduce your children to better eating habits, starting with growing a sprout garden. Teaching them by example to eat fresh foods offers them a better start in life. Kids love to watch the sprouts grow, and then they get to eat what they have seen. They don't even wait for a dressing—they just eat them. You will also be a better pet parent by supplementing your pets' food with fresh greens, beans, and grasses. Cats, dogs, birds, and other critters love to eat sprouts. Do you buy cat grass? You will find out how to grow your own for pennies. This will even give you an opportunity to be a better caretaker to yourself. It's true. Just by sprouting.

SPROUTING SAVES YOU MONEY

Follow the money! It is very economical to sprout. Beans and legumes double in size. One pound (454 g) of seeds the size of the tiny alfalfa seed will yield about 6 to 7 pounds (2.7 to 3.2 kg) of mature sprouts, for a fraction of the price of purchasing organic vegetables in that quantity. And you will save time. It only takes about a week or so to grow a full tray of speckled peas for shoots to use as a salad. Growing lettuce in the garden takes longer than that. My speckled peas grow in the tray on the counter and do not have any bugs, nor do they need weeding, and I do not need to worry about them getting ready to flower to produce seed, also known as bolting. There is rarely a storage issue, because in most cases the whole tray gets eaten just about the time the sprouts become mature. Sprouting seeds means saving money.

HOMEGROWN SPROUTS ARE SAFE

Safety first. Sprouts you grow at home are safe. Home sprouters use clean, fresh water, wash their hands before touching seeds or sprouts, and clean the sprouting containers with hot sudsy water. Do you know who touches the seeds and the sprouts? You do! When you purchase commercially grown sprouts, who knows who has been handling the package, where it has been, or for how long?

SPROUTING MEANS A GREENER FOOTPRINT FOR THE EARTH

Sprouting is carbon-friendly. There is no better way to reduce your carbon footprint than to grow your own sprouts. The sprouts do not travel in a truck to get to you, they do not require pesticides or herbicides, and they don't cause pollution. It is a very green thing to do. You can do small green things on your own that have large impacts in the world.

SPROUTING ENCOURAGES MINDFULNESS

Growing your own sprouts is very good for your body and mind. When you eat your own sprouts, your body benefits. When you take care of your sprouts, your mind benefits. Taking care of sprouts is very enjoyable and keeps your mind focused. You can use it as a meditation. Be mindful when rinsing the seeds. Be mindful while eating the sprouts. Taste the individual sprout and feel the difference between the types of sprouts against your tongue and the inside of your mouth. Be one with the sprout.

THE PERSONAL IS POLITICAL

Growing and eating your own sprouts is a very local food thing to do that has greater world implications. To grow a sprout is to grow a fresh, local food. Using organic seed for sprouting is the way to go.

SPROUTS ARE BEAUTIFUL

Sprout gardens are beautiful. It is nice to have living green things in the home. In addition to houseplants, try house sprouts to green up your home. Each leafy sprout has a different-shaped and -sized leaf. They come in a variety of shades of green, sometimes mixed with tinges of other colors like reds, purples, and yellows. The seeds come in all shapes and sizes, too, and make for beautiful organic displays in any home. You can even make art out of the seeds.

SPROUTS ARE AVAILABLE YEAR-ROUND

Homegrown sprouts are available to you all the time, all year round. You can sprout in an apartment, you can sprout in Alaska during the winter, and you can sprout on the tallest mountaintop. Your sprouts will be there for you when you need them most. No need to take a car to the vegetable market when you have sprouts on your kitchen counter.

YOU CAN FARM THE ORGANIC WAY

Choose organic seeds for sprouting and help the planet and your body by not using pesticides, herbicides, or chemical additives. By using organic seeds, you become an organic farmer in your own home while supporting those who grow the plants to maturity to harvest the seeds.

WHO SPROUTS?

People from all walks of life sprout. Every continent on this planet is home to many people who sprout. Sprouters can be found everywhere. They are sometimes elusive. You may not be able to tell they are sprouters just by looking at them, but we are here. And once you have started sprouting, once you have joined the rest of us, it is a skill and a lifestyle that will remain with you throughout your life.

SPROUTING FOR HEALTH

People who are looking for healthy foods often turn to sprouting. Pick up any newspaper or magazine, skim through health and diets books at the corner store or the library, listen to the news on the radio, or tune in to your favorite reporters on a cable network, and if there is a story about eating for health, there will be a mention of increasing your intake of vegetables. Vegetables are great sources of many of the macronutrients we need to stay alive and are void of large quantities of the types of fats and carbohydrates that we need to stay away from for good long-term health. Sprouts are vegetables in their newest form.

Diets that lower your risk of cancer include eating foods that are low in saturated fats. Seek out foods that are high in unsaturated fats or monounsaturated fats. Consume more fiber. Eat dark leafy green vegetables. Alfalfa, clover, broccoli, wheatgrass, sunflower, and buckwheat sprouts are all examples of dark leafy green vegetables that are also good sources of fiber and other macronutrients. They are a wonderful source of chlorophyll, the component that makes leaves green.

Bean and legume sprouts are a good source of protein for diabetics. Sprouted beans and legumes are easily digested and taste great. They are low in fat and high in fiber. The carbohydrates that are found in these foods are the good carbs, the types of carbs we want in our daily diets.

There are many sprouts that are gluten-free. It is actually easier to discuss the few that have gluten. Any of the hard wheat-derived grains—wheat, barley, rye, spelt, and triticale—contain gluten. Oats are often processed in the same facility as gluten-containing grains and can become contaminated with gluten during processing. Also, some people are sensitive to the peptides in the proteins that make up oats. Quinoa, amaranth, and millet are non-wheat grains and do not contain gluten. And leafy greens, shoots, legumes, and beans are gluten-free. Choices abound with sprouts!

A heart-healthy diet includes eating more vegetables, especially the dark leafy types—like sprouts! Whole grains that are a good source of fiber can help with blood pressure, and sprouted grains are a very tasty option.

Weight-loss diets can use sprouts for the feeling of fullness without the extra calories. Sprouts are high in fiber, and beans and legumes can take a while to digest, keeping your digestive tract busy without sending those "Feed me! I'm hungry!" signals. When you are hungry, turn to nutrient-rich sprouts.

Low-carb diet followers can feel great about consuming sprouts because they are the good carbs—the types of carbs that your body needs and will use up and not store as extra fat. Unprocessed, whole carbs are necessary for the body's continued good health, and sprouts offer just that.

SPROUTING FOR LIFE

Who else eats sprouts? Anyone and everyone who wants to eat fresh, homegrown vegetables. People who enjoy eating a little bit of dark leafy green veggies or those who enjoy the crunchy, sweet taste of sprouted beans and legumes. People who juice often find themselves growing quantities of sprouts to add that extra boost to their concoctions.

Demographics show that sprouters are almost equally split between male and female. There are many households that have one family member sprouting and no others. Eventually the others convert, even just once in a while, to share those tasty bites. Sprouters are ageless, but there is an above-average concentration of sprouters in their forties and fifties.

Sprouts are a great food choice for students living in dorms; people in nursing homes or assisted living facilities; people living in or traveling by boat or motor home; people on vacation or people who work; people who live in small apartments or people who live in houses that have many square feet or just a few. Some truck drivers enjoy taking their sprouters on the road so that they get fresh veggies while hauling loads. Sprouting can happen anywhere.

Vegetarians, vegans, and raw foodists are sprouters. But people who enjoy red meat, poultry, and fish can also find themselves sprouting. These fresh new vegetables lend themselves very easily to many different types of foods from various ethnic backgrounds. Sprouts on a hamburger afford a tasty alternative to lettuce that was grown perhaps hundreds of miles away. A bean sprouted salad served next to tender fish fillets delivers a contrast of taste and texture.

Enjoyed as an everyday food, sprouts never become boring. Eaten by themselves or together as an accompaniment, they are perfect for meals and snacks. And you can sprout for yourself, or to share with family, friends, neighbors, and coworkers. Come and join me on this wonderfully green and fresh adventure!

WHAT IS SPROUTING?

A sprout is a germinated seed. Germination is both a physical process and a series of chemical reactions in which the dormant seed absorbs water and turns into a live sprout. The most important step in sprouting is the soaking process. During soaking, the seed absorbs water. The water diffuses through the seed coat into the embryo, causing the seed to swell. You can sometimes actually see this by observing the cracked seed casing after soaking.

Germination of seeds with the correct amount of water and oxygen, and at the right temperature, results in the chemical reaction known as respiration, in which energy is released from glucose (simple sugar) by a series of chemical reactions. The sugar breaks down into carbon dioxide and water, and oxygen is used during the process. Respiration releases energy from food—in this case, from the sugar.

The formula for aerobic respiration is: Glucose + Oxygen = Water + Carbon Dioxide + Adensoine Triphosphate (ATP)

ATP, or energy, is used by the seed to start developing and growing into what will become a very delicious and nutritious sprout in a few days' time as plant cells duplicate. Everything a seed needs to become a sprout is right there in the seed. It only needs the absorption of water at the right temperature to change from a seed to a sprout.

What we see in sprouts like alfalfa, radish, and clover are not leaves but are called cotyledons. The first true leaves of the plant do not appear for several weeks, around day 25. The sprouts with the cotyledons are what we will eat. Grasses, on the other hand, do not have cotyledons but grow up within a hollow structure, a coleoptile. Soon after it rises above the soil line, the true leaf appears as a blade of grass.

Plants, even in the early sprout stage, produce a chemical called chlorophyll. This is what makes leaves green. They use the chlorophyll to capture energy from the sun and are able to synthesize carbohydrates from carbon dioxide and water in a process called photosynthesis.

One of the reasons we eat leafy green sprouts for our diets and/or juice the grasses is to get the chlorophyll from the sprout or grass.

All of this happens in just a few days' time. With the soaking of the seeds and the cycle of rinsing and draining, we can foster the correct environment for seeds to sprout. As enzymes help facilitate the growth of the sprout, they also help create the macro- and micronutrients that our bodies need to work properly.

Sprouting is more than the sum of its parts. It is much more than the germination of a seed through a physical process and chemical reactions. It can greatly enhance our nutrition by offering a fresh and tasty alternative to our diets. It can become a family activity that brings everyone together. People can connect to each other through sprouting. Many people feel that they are the only ones in their entire community who sprout, only to find out by some chance that there are others near them. It is an adventure that begins with a seed, some water, and you.

PART I:
WHAT YOU NEED TO START SPROUTING

CHAPTER 2:
CHOOSE YOUR SPROUTER

SPROUTERS ARE SPECIALIZED DEVICES DESIGNED
TO DO THE WORK OF SPROUTING. THESE ARE
THE TOOLS THAT YOU CAN USE TO HAVE A GREAT
SPROUTING EXPERIENCE. YOU CAN GET THE JOB OF
SPROUTING DONE WITH THE RIGHT EQUIPMENT.

THERE ARE THREE PRIMARY METHODS OF SPROUTING
AND THEIR VARIATIONS: THE JAR, THE BAG, AND
THE TRAY. WE WILL ALSO EXPLORE AUTOMATIC
SPROUTING, WHICH IS A TYPE OF TRAY SPROUTING
USING AN ELECTRIC MACHINE.

EACH METHOD HAS ITS OWN BENEFITS. EACH
METHOD HAS ITS OWN FANS.

SOME SEEDS CAN ONLY BE SPROUTED USING A
PARTICULAR METHOD, BUT WITH MOST SEEDS
YOU HAVE A CHOICE, SO IT WILL COME DOWN TO
PERSONAL PREFERENCE. YOU MAY END UP LIKING
ONLY ONE WAY OF SPROUTING AND DECIDE NOT
TO USE ANY OTHER OPTIONS. OR YOU MAY END
UP PICKING AND CHOOSING THE WAY YOU SPROUT
DEPENDING UPON WHAT YOU ARE SPROUTING OR
WHERE YOU ARE LOCATED. EXPERIMENT WITH THE
DIFFERENT SPROUTERS FOR YOURSELF AND FIND
ONE OR MORE THAT ARE BEST SUITED TO YOU.

JAR SPROUTER

One of the most widely popular methods of sprouting is the glass mason jar. It is an affordable and easy way to begin. In fact, it is often the first method of sprouting for many people. Found new in general merchandise stores, mason jars can also be purchased used at garage and yard sales, rummage sales, flea markets, and collectible shops.

You can soak and sprout seeds all in the same jar. And now there are different ways to make jar sprouting even easier. Because this method has less air circulation than other ways to sprout, using a stainless steel screen or plastic mesh lid helps with proper drainage and keeps the air circulating more

than if the opening were completely covered. Mason jar sprouting is a popular method to use because glass is a more natural product than the plastic from which many sprouters are manufactured.

There are some drawbacks to sprouting with jars, however. The biggest one is the lack of air, which creates the perfect environment for growing mold and mildew. This can be mitigated with the help of stainless steel screens and plastic mesh lids. These tools also help with drainage when the jar is correctly positioned to let the water from rinsing flow out.

Not all seeds can be jar sprouted. The larger ones, such as sunflower, buckwheat, pea shoots, and the grasses, all need to be done in a tray sprouter. Arugula, cress, flax, and chia do not sprout at all in jars because the gel-like substance that surrounds the seed in the presence of water does not allow them to sprout properly, so they just rot.

If you look outside you see grass, trees, shrubbery, and flowers that all began as some sort of seed. They grow up straight and tall. Seeds sprouted in jars do not grow up straight and tall, as Mother Nature intended. Jar sprouting prevents this from happening and the sprouts grow around each other in a tangled ball.

This is not to say that sprouting cannot be done in jars. The small leafy green sprouts, beans, and grains can be sprouted in jars very nicely. For some, it is the only way to sprout, and it is a method that has served them well with their favorite seeds.

If you go this route, choose a wide-mouth mason jar. This will allow more and better air circulation around the sprouts, which will help protect them from mold. Also, if you choose to use a stainless steel screen or plastic mesh lid, these tools are manufactured to fit a wide-mouth mason jar.

If you use a screen, the screen replaces the flat part of the lid-and-ring closure for canning. You will need to provide the ring and use the screen in place of the flat lid. The plastic mesh lid is both the lid and the ring in one piece. There is no need to supply anything else.

BASIC DIRECTIONS:

Soak the seeds overnight in the jar and in the morning drain out the water so that you have only wet seeds in the jar. Rinse with fresh water and drain that out. Rinse and drain two times each day, once in the morning and once in the evening, making sure you drain out all of the excess water so that you are left with only wet seeds/sprouts in the jar and no standing water. While you are rinsing the sprouts remember that you are the sprout farmer, that you are everything to those sprouts. In essence, you are Mother Nature for them. Do not rush through the rinsing process, but allow them some time to soak up the water. Sprouts like to take baths; it makes them feel invigorated, refreshed, and ready to grow. Go and brush your teeth or comb your hair to give them a few moments in the water.

Once the sprouts are mature, you can eat them. One of the benefits of jar sprouting is that you can store the sprouts in the jar in the refrigerator. Simply cover the top with an airtight lid and the sprouts can stay fresh for about one week. Give them a nice bath every few days and drain well. A system of two jars that alternate between growing sprouts and storing sprouts will allow you to eat fresh sprouts every day.

Cleaning the mason jar is as simple as washing it with warm sudsy water and rinsing with hot water. These are dishwasher-safe even when using the pot-scrubber or sanitize cycles.

THE EASY SPROUTER

The Easy Sprouter is a variation on jar sprouting that makes this system work much better. It has an outer container and a smaller vented inner container that creates air circulation to decrease the chances of growing mold and mildew while cultivating fresh, great-tasting sprouts.

Everything you need to sprout is here. There is a measuring cup for measuring the dry seeds before sprouting. It can also be used for measuring mature sprouts to get ready for sprout-related recipes. You can soak the seeds in the inner container and just pull it out to drain and rinse. The system comes with two lids—vented and non-vented—for sprouting and for storing the mature sprouts. The Easy Sprouter uses the natural heat generated by the growing sprouts to keep them warm and moist enough to grow without needing an excessive amount of rinsing and draining.

Traveling with sprouts is not always an easy task, but this method of sprouting changes that. Take your sprouts on the road with you to work or play or far away. The Easy Sprouter was designed to be a self-contained unit that travels easily, so there is no excuse for not having fresh sprouts with you every day, even if you are not near your own home.

BASIC DIRECTIONS:

After measuring the seeds in the measuring cup, put them into the vented inner container and put that into the solid outer container. Fill the container with water to soak the seeds overnight. In the morning, lift out the inner container and let the water drain away. Discard the soaking water. Rinse the seeds/sprouts with fresh water and put the inner container back into the outer container. Do this two times each day, once in the morning and once in the evening, making sure you leave only wet seeds/sprouts. There should be no standing water in the Easy Sprouter. While you are rinsing the sprouts, remember that you are the sprout farmer, that you are everything to those sprouts. In essence, you are Mother Nature for them. Do not rush through the rinsing process, but allow them some time to soak up the water. Sprouts like to take baths; it makes them feel invigorated, refreshed, and ready to grow. Go and brush your teeth or comb your hair to give them a few moments in the water.

In a few days' time, the quart-sized container will have mature sprouts ready to eat. Storing mature sprouts is easy to do and doesn't require anything other than the Easy Sprouter. You can store them in the sprouter in the refrigerator until you are ready to eat them. A system of two Easy Sprouters that alternates between growing sprouts and storing sprouts will allow fresh sprouts to be eaten every day.

It is easy to use and easy to clean. Using the top rack in the dishwasher and a hot water rinse, or a washing in the sink with warm soapy water, keeps the Easy Sprouter ready for use when you next want to sprout some seeds.

HEMP SPROUTING BAG

Sprouting beans, legumes, and grains in a hemp sprouting bag is a refreshing endeavor. The hemp bag is able to keep the sprouts moist enough between rinses while simultaneously allowing aeration. You can sprout with the bag and not worry about mold or mildew building up because the fibers allow for air circulation.

Hemp material is well known for its strength and durability. It will not lose its shape even after repeated use, and it will typically soften over time. It is also naturally resistant to mold when used correctly. Flax has the same qualities as hemp and also makes nice sprouting bags.

Hemp sprouting bags are easy to use and portable, too. Take bags with you to work for fresh sprouts at lunchtime or a snack break. Pack them on your next hike or bike ride. They go anywhere you go and provide a nourishing food source. You can eat the mature sprouts directly from the bag.

Generally, beans, legumes, and grains will about double in size after sprouting. If you want 1 cup (50 g) of mature sprouts, start with 1/2 cup (50 g) of dry seed or grain. Soak the seeds in a jar or bowl of water overnight. You will need more than three times the amount of water as seed because these types of seed absorb a large quantity of water compared to their size.

BASIC DIRECTIONS:

Prepare the bag by soaking it in water for a few minutes. This will get it ready for the seeds. Pour the soaked seeds into the bag over a sink. Let the water drain out, then rinse with fresh water, and allow that water to drain out. Pull the drawstring closed, and then hang the bag somewhere so it can drip. Always hang the bag; never put it on a flat surface like a plate, counter, or dish rack. If the bag lies on a flat surface, the seeds will rot.

Rinse the seeds two times each day with fresh water, once in the morning and once in the evening, allowing the water to drain out, and then hang to drip. After you have rinsed the seeds, you can massage the bag. The massaging action prevents the roots from taking hold of the bag's fibers and helps with air circulation.

While you are rinsing the sprouts remember that you are the sprout farmer, that you are everything to those sprouts. In essence, you are Mother Nature for them. Do not rush through the rinsing process, but allow them some time to soak up the water. Sprouts like to take baths; it makes them feel invigorated, refreshed, and ready to grow. You can put the bag in a sink or bowl of water and let it stay there for a minute or two to soak up the water instead of running the tap water.

You can store the mature sprouts in the bag in the fridge. While they are in the fridge, rinse them every few days with fresh water. A nice bath keeps them alive and healthy and prevents them from drying out.

CARING FOR YOUR HEMP BAG

Hemp sprouting bags can last for many years of continuous use when cared for properly. After each sprouting session, you can simply rinse the bag in hot water, hang it to dry, and then start all over again. If you feel you need to wash it, use a mild soap, something you might use for a baby's clothes—there's no need for detergent. Wash in warm sudsy water, rinse in hot water, and hang to dry. Drying outside in the sun will help keep bacteria away.

Staining of the bag is natural; the stain comes from the seeds and not mold or mildew. Dyeing cloth with vegetables is an old-fashioned process that was once widely used. Drying the bags in the sunlight or boiling them in water will help lighten the stain naturally.

SPROUTING TRAYS

Tray sprouting is a very easy way to sprout and there are many different brands of tray sprouters available on the market. Professional sprout growers and wheatgrass growers use the tray method of sprouting. They all have some similar attributes, but you should always follow the manufacturer's directions.

Most tray sprouters are made from plastic. Some brands are rectangles and some are round. There are those that stack and there are tray sprouters that are one layer. Tray sprouters can sprout a wide variety of seeds, beans, and legumes conveniently and quickly. The trays themselves have holes in the bottom to let the water drain out and for air circulation. Look for trays that are made from food-grade plastic and are BPA-free.

These sprouters work on the greenhouse effect principle and come with lids or closed systems with ventilation to keep in the moisture so that the new sprouts can grow without drying out between rinsing cycles. Sprouting in trays allows the seeds to grow straight up and tall, the way Mother Nature intended plants of all sorts to grow. For a small amount of space, a volume amount of sprouting can be done that guarantees fresh sprouts can be eaten on a daily basis.

BASIC DIRECTIONS:

Soak the seeds in a jar or bowl of water overnight. (Some tray sprouters do not require an overnight soak.) Pour the seeds into the sprouter over a sink. Let the water drain out, then rinse with fresh water and let that water drain out so that you have only wet seeds in the tray. Put the lid on the tray. Rinse and drain the seeds two times each day, once in the morning and once in the evening, draining out the excess water. While you are rinsing the sprouts, remember that you are the sprout farmer, that you are everything to those sprouts. In essence, you are Mother Nature for them. Do not rush through the rinsing process, but allow them some time to soak up the water. Sprouts like to take baths; it makes them feel invigorated, refreshed, and ready to grow. Sing them a little song.

Wash the sprouter in warm sudsy water and rinse with hot water. Some are dishwasher-safe on the top rack, but check the manufacturer's directions before attempting this. The hulls from the seeds often get stuck in the holes of the tray. A gentle scrubbing will release them, but if that does not work an opened paper clip can be used to pop the holes clear.

Some tray sprouters can be used to store the mature sprouts in the refrigerator until they are eaten. With others, you need to take the mature sprouts out and store them in a different container.

TERRA–COTTA CLAY SPROUTING TRAY

Using a terra-cotta clay sprouter is possibly the nicest way to sprout. The clay's absorbent qualities mimic the conditions of soil and help keep the sprouts hydrated and ventilated throughout the day between rinsings. It also keeps the sprouts cooler as their temperature rises during the growing process.

Choose a clay sprouter that is lead-free and does not contain cadmium. You need to look for untreated and unglazed clay for the sprouts. A lead-free glazed tray at the bottom to catch the water drippings is common, but the trays for sprouting should not be glazed.

This method of sprouting can be used for all seeds, including the tiny leafy sprouts like alfalfa, clover, radish, and broccoli. Beans and legumes like the trays. You can use them for sunflower, buckwheat, and pea shoots. Although wheatgrass and barley grass would grow fine in the trays, they are usually small in size and will not grow a large amount of grass or enough to get even an ounce (30 ml) of juice.

The clay sprouter truly excels at sprouting the gelatinous seeds—chia, cress, arugula, and flax. These seeds form a gel-like sac around the seed in the presence of water. The clay acts like soil and absorbs the gooey material so that the seeds can sprout as usual.

If you are using the trays to sprout these seeds, do not presoak them. When wet, the seeds are difficult to manage. Sprinkle them on the tray dry and rinse with fresh water, letting the water drain out so that you are left with wet seeds in the tray. Rinse and drain two times each day, making sure you let the excess water drain out.

BASIC DIRECTIONS:

For gelationous seeds like chia, arugula, flax, cress, and psyllium, sprinkle the dry seeds onto the already soaked tray. For other seeds, soak your seeds in a jar or bowl of water overnight as usual. Then, soak the tray in water for about 15 to 30 minutes, so that it can absorb water. Pour the soaked seeds into the tray, letting the excess water drain out. This happens slowly because some of the water will pass through the tray. You can do this in a sink and let it sit for a few minutes until all of the water has drained out. Now rinse again with fresh water, letting all of the excess water drain away so that you are left with only wet seeds in the sprouter. Put the lid on the tray. The lid helps create a greenhouse effect and keeps everything moist and from drying out. Rinse the seeds two times each day, once in the morning and once in the evening, being certain to let the excess water drain out so that you only have wet seeds or sprouts in the tray.

If your terra-cotta clay sprouter comes with several trays, then you can start a new tray each day or every other day so that you create a rotation of trays. This will allow you to have fresh sprouts on a continuous basis.

When the small leafy green sprouts are mature, take off the lid and put the tray in a sunny spot. Do not use direct sunlight; any ordinary daylight that comes in the room is fine. They will green up with chlorophyll in a few hours. When the larger leafy green sprouts hit the top of the lid, take it off and let them sprout a few days longer. They will not dry out because their root system is now large enough.

You can use a soft scrub brush to clean the trays after sprouting. Sometimes the tiny holes get filled up with the leftover seeds. Use an unbent paper clip to pop them through so that the holes are empty and ready for the next batch of seeds.

WHEATGRASS AND BARLEY GRASS TRAYS

Homegrown wheatgrass and barley grass can be done effectively and economically and affords a freshness of grass that is second to none. Drinking the juice from wheatgrass or barley grass that you have grown yourself tastes great and gives your body the nutrients and chlorophyll it needs to work and feel better. This process does take a commitment of time and space, but in the end you can drink the freshest wheatgrass or barley grass juice available because you grew it yourself.

There are two ways to grow the grass—with soil and without soil. Aside from using fertilizer for the non-soil method, the final nutritional profiles are very similar, and there is a slightly milder taste to the hydroponically grown grass. It comes down to personal choice for either method. A good idea may be to grow some grass each way and find out for yourself which one works best for you.

Wheatgrass and barley grass are best grown in a tray sprouter. Because the blades of grass need to grow tall, they do not do well in jars. The grass for juice can also be grown in automatic sprouters. You need a large amount of wheatgrass or barley grass to get a small amount of juice. Professional grass growers have trays that measure 10 x 20 inches (25 x 51 cm)—these are known as standard nursery flats. You may have seen similar trays if you have ever gone to a nursery. A tray of this size will yield about 8 ounces (235 ml) of juice.

Sunflower sprouts, whole buckwheat for greens, and peas for shoots can also be sprouted in the trays. The sprouts from these seeds are often used for juicing, in which case you need a large amount of sprouts to produce a small amount of juice. They can be eaten and are the basis for salads replacing lettuce. There is almost nothing better than to build a sprout salad on a bed of fresh, homegrown pea shoots. It's sweet, crunchy, and delicious.

For basic health maintenance, the dosage is 2 to 4 ounces (60 to 120 ml) each day of either wheatgrass or barley grass juice, 1 or 2 ounces (30 or 60 ml) in the morning and 1 or 2 ounces (30 or 60 ml) in the evening on an empty stomach, 30 minutes before you eat or drink anything. Therapeutic dosages start at 8 ounces (235 ml) per day.

One 10 x 20-inch (25 x 51 cm) tray will yield two to four days' worth of grass. In order to have a continual supply of the juice you may need to have several trays growing at one time, each at a different stage, so that you have a rotation of trays, some in the beginning growth stage, some in the middle, and some ready to juice. Do not start at a large dosage. Start small to see how your body tolerates the juice, then slowly build up to larger doses.

The 10 x 20-inch (25 x 51 cm) trays come with holes and without holes. The seeds go into the trays with holes, and that tray fits into the solid tray to avoid dripping water or soil in the home. It is also possible to get clear plastic humidity domes that fit over the trays to create a greenhouse effect to prevent the new grass from drying out.

If you choose to use soil, use a good-quality soil. The already mixed potting soils available at garden centers and nurseries are a good choice. You may be able to find soil that has peat moss or other aerators to keep the soil light and enable good drainage. Compost from decaying food or worm compost added to the soil is a great plus.

You can also choose not to use soil. Some sort of growing medium is beneficial when growing the grass hydroponically because it keeps the grass from drying out too much in between waterings and gives the roots a place to grow. Growing mediums for grass come in a variety of forms, such as vermiculite, perlite, coconut coir, recycled PET plastic, and cellulose fibers.

Because the grass grows for a longer amount of time than sprouts do, usually around ten days, it is a good idea to use fertilizer to help it along the way. Fertilizer can be added during the soaking time. It can also be sprayed onto the root area of the grass after it has been rinsed. See page 48 for more information about fertilizer.

BASIC DIRECTIONS FOR GROWING HYDROPONIC WHEATGRASS OR BARLEY GRASS:

Soak the seeds in a jar or bowl of water overnight. If you are using a growing medium, place the medium in the tray with the holes. Pour the seeds into the tray, letting the water drain out. Rinse the seeds with fresh water and let that drain away. There should be only wet seeds and the growing medium left in the tray and no standing water. Place the humidity dome on top of the tray. Twice each day, once in the morning and once in the evening, rinse and drain the seeds/sprouts, making sure there is no standing water. The grass is ready to juice in about ten days.

BASIC DIRECTIONS FOR GROWING WHEATGRASS AND BARLEY GRASS IN SOIL:

Soak the seeds in a jar or bowl of water overnight. Put soil into the tray with holes. You do not need a lot of soil, maybe just 1 inch (2.5 cm) or so. Drain out the water from the seeds and plant the soaked seeds in the soil. Cover the seeds with a thin layer of soil, 1/8 inch (3 mm) or so. This will keep them from drying out. Keep the soil moist but not soaking wet. The grass is ready to juice in about ten days.

Keep the trays clean after each use by washing them in warm sudsy water and rinsing with hot water. You can usually get two cuttings of grass out of one planting, so you would need to clean the trays after the second cutting of the grass. Composting the soil if possible is a good idea.

Ordinary fruit and vegetable juicers will not juice the grass. The grass blades will wrap themselves around the cutting mechanism of the juicer and will burn out the motor. Wheatgrass juicers have an auger, which looks like a big screw. The blades of grass are wrapped around the inside and then are squeezed to release the juice.

Wheatgrass juicers come in two types: manual and electric. Manual juicers are not as expensive as the electric ones, but they take more time and energy to use. Look for stainless steel manual juicers, which are easy to keep clean and more hygienic. There are many choices for electric juicers and careful study will allow you to find one that fits your needs and pocketbook.

High-speed blenders can be used in place of a juicer. Cut the blades of grass into smaller 1- or 2-inch (2.5 or 5 cm) pieces. Pour about 1 cup (235 ml) of water into the container, then add the grass. After blending, you can strain the solids to produce a nice, easy-to-drink green juice. This method does produce a lot of heat and can oxidize the grass. It produces a diluted grass juice because of the added water.

If you do not like the taste of the juice, you can mix it. Try to mix the juice with other green leafy veggies. Try celery, spinach, or sprouts like alfalfa, clover, or broccoli. Radish or mustard sprouts will give the grass a little bit of a kick. When you mix the grass with fruit it becomes less effective for the body. This can be a great and satisfying adventure. With practice and patience, homegrown wheatgrass or barley grass juice can be yours ready to drink.

THE EASYGREEN AUTOMATIC SPROUTING TRAY

Automatic machines take sprouting to an entirely different level for both novice and veteran sprouters. These tools take away the daily exercise of rinsing and draining the sprouts. They help provide a continuous supply of fresh, homegrown sprouts. A quick search on the Internet will show a variety of electric automatic sprouters, including those that you can make yourself from easily acquired items. The EasyGreen Automatic Sprouter uses a patented misting system to keep the seeds and sprouts hydrated throughout the day so they do not become dry. This system completely eliminates the need for the overnight presoak for seeds because they are misted continuously at predetermined intervals. The twice-daily procedure of rinsing and draining is no longer needed. The excess water drains away from the machine through holes in the trays.

The system also oxygenates the seeds, which is an important part of the germination process. Even outdoor garden seeds that have been planted in soil need oxygen. That is why seeds planted in a garden do better in well-aerated soils and one of the reasons why earthworms are so important to gardening.

Sprouts need the correct temperature to grow properly, and the EasyGreen Automatic Sprouter helps maintain this temperature. As they grow, sprouts create heat and the daily cycle of rinsing and draining of the growing sprouts not only hydrates but also cools them. The automatic rinsings keep the growing sprouts cool and moist.

Notice that the water reservoir is in the back of the machine and the sprouts are in the cavity in the front of the machine. The wastewater drains away after the misting so that only fresh water touches the sprouts and not recycled water. Some automatic sprouters have the water reservoir below the seeds and the water is reused as it is circulated from the bottom to the top by the pump. Reused and recirculated water in a warm plastic

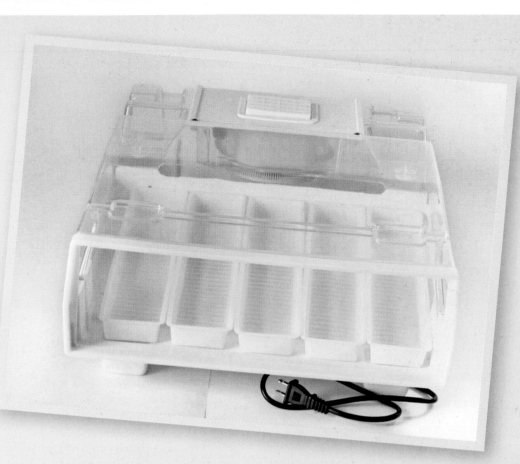

environment is the perfect place to grow bacteria. The EasyGreen Automatic Sprouter allows only fresh water to touch the sprouts, not reused or recirculated water.

The cavity of the machine houses the trays that hold the seeds. You can grow your sprouts in five cartridges, in ten junior cartridges, or for volume sprouting of wheatgrass, sunflowers, buckwheat, or pea shoots, in a tray that fills the entire inside section of the machine.

Using an automatic machine does have an additional cost component compared with any of the manual methods of sprouting. But for many people that cost can be overlooked by the convenience of the method and the consistent outcome of the sprouts due to the regular cycles of rinsing and draining the sprouts receive. Over the life of the machine with the amount of sprouts that it will produce, the initial investment can save money.

BASIC DIRECTIONS:

It is always wise to follow the exact directions from the manufacturer. Set up the machine according to the manufacturer's instructions. This will include but is not limited to setting up the component parts of the machine, filling the reservoir with water, preparing the drainage tube, and getting the timer ready. Once the machine is all set to use, place dry seeds in the cartridges or trays depending upon what you are sprouting. Plug the machine into the wall socket and it will commence the misting of the seeds. This will occur at regularly selected intervals throughout the day. You will usually need to fill the reservoir with fresh water once a day. No watering and draining of the growing sprouts need to be done by you. The machine takes over from here as long as you keep the water reservoir filled with water.

Fresh mature sprouts will be ready in a few days' time, often sooner than with manual methods due to the regular rinsing cycles. Using a rotation of the five cartridges or ten junior cartridges will give you fresh, tasty sprouts every day, in an amount that you can consume on a daily basis. When you have eaten the sprouts on a cartridge, wash it, and then use it again. Growing a volume amount of sprouts or grasses in the larger trays is also an option.

Cleaning the machine is almost as easy as growing the sprouts. You can use some bleach or any green type of cleaner in the water reservoir. Remove all sprouts from the cavity, put the machine on, and it cleans itself, automatically.

WHICH SPROUTER IS BEST FOR YOU?

AS WE SAW IN THE PREVIOUS CHAPTER, THERE ARE THREE WAYS TO SPROUT: JARS, TRAYS, AND BAGS. THE FIRST TWO METHODS HAVE SOME VARIATIONS. MANY PEOPLE LEARNED TO SPROUT USING A MASON JAR AND SOME OF US SPROUTERS LEARNED USING A TRAY. JAR LOVERS AND TRAY LOVERS ARE EVERYWHERE. DONE CORRECTLY, THESE WAYS OF SPROUTING CAN PROVIDE GREAT AMOUNTS OF TASTY SPROUTS. SO WHAT ARE THE DIFFERENCES?

JAR	TRAY	BAG
Leafy sprouts grow around each other in a tangled ball of roots and stems. Beans and grains with their shorter growing times do well in jars.	Leafy sprouts grow straight up and down like an oak tree. Beans and grains with their shorter growing times do well in trays.	Leafy sprouts are not suitable for bag sprouting. Beans and grains do very well in bags.
Used to sprout beans and grains for a short time. Can also be used for small leafy green seeds.	Used for all types of seeds—beans, grains, and leafy greens.	Used to sprout beans and grains for a short period of time.
Greater chance for mold and mildew at the bottom of the jar.	Less chance of mold and mildew with greater air circulation.	Great air circulation without drying out the sprouts and minimal chance of mold or mildew.
Individual jars do not take up much space.	Takes up more room than a jar.	Bags do not take up much room and should be hung.
Not all leafy sprouts get to see daylight—just the ones at the very top.	All leafy sprouts can stretch and grow tall to reach the light.	Leafy sprouts won't get enough light. Beans and grains do not need the light to grow.
Sprouts get watered from the top and drainage occurs at the top by putting the jar upside down at an angle.	Sprouts get watered from the top and the water drains out the bottom.	Sprouts get watered from all over and also receive an enjoyable massage.
Plastic jar sprouters travel well.	It is not always easy to travel with tray sprouters.	Bag sprouters travel very easily to work or play.
Cannot sprout the gelatinous seeds, grasses, or shoots.	Able to sprout gelatinous seeds, grasses, and shoots.	Can sprout gelatinous seeds on top of the bag. Not good for grasses or shoots.

You can choose which method works best for your own situation, and you can mix up the methods depending on which seeds you are sprouting.

CHAPTER 3:
SEEDS, BEANS, AND LEGUMES... OH, MY!

SPROUTING IS MOSTLY A PROCESS OF SOAKING, RINSING, AND DRAINING SEEDS. SOME ELEMENTS OF SPROUTING, SUCH AS SEED CHOICE, SAFE FOOD-HANDLING PRACTICES, WHICH SPROUTER TO USE, AND HOW TO AVOID MOLD, CAN BENEFIT FROM FURTHER DISCUSSION.

ALL ABOUT SEEDS

As with any endeavor, the more you know, the better your product will be. There is a lot to know about seed, but it is not overwhelming or overly scientific. You'll need to know about the benefits of getting organic seed, seed toxins, mixing and storing seed, and optimal seed sprouting temperatures.

ORGANIC SEEDS

The best homegrown sprouts start with good-quality organic sprouting seeds. When we grow our sprouts and eat them with our family and friends, we want nutritious, great-tasting sprouts, but we also want to make sure they started from organic seed.

Farmers grow crops to maturity and harvest them so that we can eat the vegetables. A broccoli farmer grows the broccoli plant from seed and at the end of the maturation cycle is able to harvest a broccoli head that we can purchase at our local store. For many farmers, that is the end of what they do. But there are farms that grow plants past the maturation point so that the plant goes to seed.

If we were to take that same head of broccoli purchased at the store and look at it, what we see is really a cluster of immature flowers. If you take that broccoli and let it stay at the farm, not harvested, each of those little bumps would become a yellow flower and each little yellow flower will produce seed. These seeds will go back into plant production on a farm, some will be used as animal feed, and some will be sold for us home sprouters.

Farms that do not follow organic practices use synthetic pesticides, herbicides, fertilizers, and fungicides. These are petroleum based. The plants from these farms absorb these chemicals. On farms that produce seeds, the plant is in the ground is for an even longer period and there is a greater opportunity for the absorption of these additives.

From the time of seed planting to the harvesting of either the vegetable that goes to the store or the seed that goes back into production or into sprouting, many applications of the petroleum-based synthetic additives have been used. Plants grown with this method of farming cannot fight off bugs, weeds, or disease on their own, so they need more of the artificial inputs.

Organically grown plants are planted in organic soil and under conditions that are approved of by local and federal certifying agencies using a set of regulated guidelines. These plants can fight off bugs, weeds, and disease and still grow to maturity. It all begins with healthy organic soil and healthy organic seeds.

For us home sprouters, we want to eat sprouts that come from organic seeds so that we are not ingesting the pesticides, herbicides, fertilizers, and fungicides used on farms that do not follow the organic regulations. Why would we want that stuff inside of us? Our purchasing dollars for organic sprouting seeds support farms that grow organically. Together, there are a great number of farmers in North America that grow organic vegetables for market and are in seed production. Often these farms are run by families that rely on the farm for income, and they also create jobs.

Seeds are specifically selected for sprouting based upon their high germination rates. While they are being processed through harvesting and cleaning, sprouting seeds are handled as if they were a fresh vegetable like a head of lettuce, in contrast to seeds that will go back into production on a farm or for animal feed, which are handled like other agricultural products not for human consumption. The seeds should be tested for salmonella, *E. coli*, listeria, and other organisms so that at the point of testing they are bacteria-free.

What's the difference between seeds purchased at the store in the bulk bin or prepackaged, and seeds for sprouting? Seeds that are specifically selected for sprouting need to be fresh because germination rates go down with time and temperature, and sprouting seeds should be tested for bacteria. Seeds purchased in bulk bins or prepackaged do not need to be fresh because they are often sold to be cooked, and because they may be cooked, there is no need to test for bacteria.

SEED TOXINS

All seeds have toxins in them, from the small alfalfa seed to watermelon seeds and acorns. This is the way Mother Nature protects herself. If seeds did not have toxins in them, then they would be defenseless against such things as bacteria, fungus, and being eaten by animals. There would be no future plants.

Toxins are sprouted away. This is why we are able to eat the sprout and not get sick. The small seeds have small amounts of toxins and the larger seeds have greater amounts of toxins. Some people exhibit stomach sensitivity when eating larger beans such as green pea and soy. This is partly due to the amount of protein and starch in these seeds, which can be more difficult for some people to digest. If any sprout gives you any stomach distress at all, then don't eat that sprout. Sometimes gently cooking a sprouted bean or legume will help with digestion. Just a few minutes in a stir-fry or hot bowl of soup will be enough to make them more digestible. If these methods still do not work, then don't eat that sprout. There are plenty of others from which to choose.

MIXING SEEDS

It is easy and tasty to mix seeds together. Contrasting seed colors and sizes in a mix is aesthetically pleasing. Some mixes have almost the same colors in the seeds with slight variations, and that looks pretty, too. Round peas and beans can be mixed with oblong mung and adzuki bean.

There is a bit of a formula to mixing seeds. First, the seeds in the mix should have similar maturation dates. Mixes are successful when all of the seeds are ready to eat on or about the same day; otherwise, you may be eating immature sprouts that have no taste or overly mature sprouts that have no nutrition.

Second, and as a bonus, raw seed mixes can make beautiful combinations. Dark seeds with light seeds, large ones with small ones, all different colors, and even seeds that have the same color can mix well together.

Finally, the mix should be tested and tasted. Do you like the feel inside your mouth? Do the sprouts taste good together? Did you use a little hot radish and some sweet clover for contrast? Is it all too sweet or too spicy?

These rules, like so many, were made to be broken. Do not be afraid of mixing seeds that have different maturation dates. If it is only by a day or so, then it may not matter very much. Lentils, when sprouted, take only about two days to maturation. When in a mix with alfalfa, clover, and radish, they will be sprouted longer to match the other leafy green seeds. The taste of the lentils mixed with the other seeds is great and still nutritious.

Gelatinous seeds like chia, flax, arugula, and cress mix well together and can be mixed with other seeds in small quantities. If you are going to mix these seeds with the non-gelatinous variety, make sure they are only about 15 to 25 percent of the total mixture. The gel-like substance that forms around the seed in the presence of water will spread over the other seeds in a very thin layer and still allow them to sprout. Too many of these seeds, however, and none at all will sprout.

Buckwheat and sunflower mix well together, but not so much with other seeds due to their longer maturation dates and the length of the sprouts. The different types of grains for grasses mix well together to make a grass mix. Grains that are sprouted for a day or two can mix with beans and legumes for a chewy, sweet sensation. Radishes and mustards add a bit of heat and spice to milder, sweet sprouts. If you enjoy a sprout on its own, you may like it in a mix with other seeds. Mixes are also a good way to get a variety of different types of sprouts for good nutrition.

PUMPKIN, SESAME, SUNFLOWER, AND NUTS

Sprouters eat some seeds because they are a good unprocessed source of particular nutrients. Good fats and proteins are readily accessible in shelled pumpkin seeds, sesame seeds (hulled and unhulled), shelled sunflower seeds, and some nuts. These seeds will not sprout into something that is green and you will not always see any change, but they help complete a diet that includes a wide variety of sprouts.

Shelled pumpkin seeds, shelled sunflower seeds, nuts, and hulled sesame seeds do not have their outer shells and, therefore, will not produce a leafy green sprout. For easier digestion they should be soaked overnight in a jar or bowl of water. The rinsing water should be drained out and the seeds or nuts

rinsed again with fresh water, with a final draining so that only wet seeds or nuts are left without any standing water. In this way, the seeds absorb water and through this physical process a chemical reaction starts that allows the proteins to break down into amino acids and the fats to break down into fatty acids for easier digestion.

Hulled sesame seeds are a yellowish white color. Unhulled sesame seeds are a darker tan. Some people enjoy the taste of hulled sesame seeds when making nut milks or butters, but it is the unhulled sesame seeds that will sprout. Keep it a very short sprouting time after the soak, about a day or so, or they will turn bitter. Either type of seed makes a nice crunchy addition to top salads or soups. Shelled sunflower seeds are silver in color and sprout in just a few days into a small silvery, crunchy sprout. These are not the larger

green sprouts you can harvest from growing sunflower seeds in the black shell. They do not have any chlorophyll, but they add a different type of nutrition, flavor, and texture to any dish. Try them with some seasoning on them instead of reaching for chips and dip.

Pumpkin seeds that have been shelled are green in color and are delicious when soaked and sprouted. Soaking them overnight can aid in digestion. You can dry-roast the seeds (not soaked) in a skillet without any oil for several minutes; they will pop as they cook and turn a little brown. Dress them up with some tamari for a great-tasting treat to be enjoyed by all. This also works with unsoaked sunflower seeds.

Nuts will not sprout but can be soaked overnight for easier digestion. Soaking often makes them a bit sweeter as well.

STORING SEEDS

Seeds should be stored at 60°F (15.6°C) or below. Storing seeds in the refrigerator or freezer is fine. Refrigerators are typically set above 32°F (0°C), frequently at 40°F (4.4°C), and freezers at 0°F (-17.8°C). Either one of these methods will work. Seeds stored properly at these temperatures will last for about one or two years. Germination rates go down with time and temperature. Storing seeds in a pantry or kitchen closet may bring bugs (especially if they are organic seeds), and the germination rates will go down over time.

You can store seeds in plastic or glass. Vacuum-sealed bags also work well. But the true key to long-term storage of seeds for sprouting is to keep them at or below 60°F (15.6°C).

If you have seeds, either old or new, and you want to find out whether they will sprout, you can test them. Count out 100 seeds and put them on a wet paper towel. Keep the paper towel moist but not soaking for a few days. The seeds will absorb the water and start to sprout. Count out how many seeds sprouted and find your germination rate. If 90 seeds sprouted, then you have a 90 percent germination rate; if 65 seeds sprouted then you have a 65 percent germination rate. You want to keep seeds at about the 80 percent germination rate. The seeds that don't sprout will rot and that will make the ones that do sprout rot along with them.

BIG BATCH AND SMALL BATCH SPROUTING

WHICH DO YOU CHOOSE, BIG BATCH SPROUTING OR SMALL BATCH SPROUTING? AND HOW DOES THIS AFFECT THE SPROUTING LIFE? SOME PEOPLE ENJOY SMALL BATCH SPROUTING. BUT THERE ARE MERITS TO BIG BATCH SPROUTING, AND THE TWO METHODS CAN BE MIXED AND MATCHED THROUGH THE WEEK.

The small batch sprouting method works best for many families and individuals. There is a certain amount of timely attention the sprouts need on a daily basis. It needs a rhythm to keep the small batches coordinated. Simply start some on Monday, another little bit on Tuesday, and some more on Wednesday, and by then the ones started on Monday are beginning to peek through and to start to show if they are the leafy kind of sprout. But if Monday's batch also had sprouting seeds that were beans or legumes, then they are perfect for lunch and some dinner on Tuesday. With small batch sprouting there is a chance to taste a variety of sprouts here and some different ones there, and they are all fresh.

Big batch sprouting works out better for others. There is little time in the day to pay attention to small amounts of sprouts in jars or trays. The timing of large batch sprouting makes the process an easier flow.

Start a whole bunch of beans or legumes on Friday and you are eating them by Monday and all during the week, because they can be refrigerated once they have reached maturity. Even sprouting the shoots can make more sense when done in large batches. Sprouting speckled peas for shoots in large batches works well because they are often the basis of salads or can be juiced in quantity. Of course, the grasses call for big batch sprouting because it takes a large amount of grass to make a small amount of juice.

Even sprouting the smaller green leafy sprouts like alfalfa, clover, broccoli, and radish, or any of the leafy green mixes, can make more sense in larger batches because they are the basis for salads and can be added to sandwiches throughout the week.

The choice for big batch sprouting or small batch sprouting is really a choice of timing and need. It depends on how you handle your sprouting schedule. There's no need to commit to one way; you can do some seeds as a small batch and others as a big batch. The important thing to do, though, is to start sprouting.

CARE AND FEEDING OF YOUR SPROUTS

Growing sprouts need a little attention to get them to maturity and ready to eat. Caring for them will yield abundant harvests.

LIGHT

Mature plants grown indoors either hydroponically or in soil usually need some sort of special lighting. There is an entire industry dedicated to lighting for this use. Different types of bulbs with varied energy outputs exist to grow specialty houseplants. If you are interested in growing fully matured vegetables indoors, that takes a whole distinct setup separate from growing regular houseplants. Hydroponic growers are especially aware of lighting. The heat from the lamps needs to be handled in a special way and reflectors are used to increase or decrease what light is available. Timers are especially useful during the growing stage.

The good news for us sprouters is that any ordinary daylight that comes into a room is fine. There is no need for any special purchase of lighting equipment. When the leafy sprouts are mature and ready to eat, just set them in a sunny room, and in a few hours they will be green with chlorophyll. Ambient daylight will take care of their needs.

Do not put the growing sprouts in direct sunlight because this will effectively cook them and they will die. Actually, growing sprouts do not need any light at all. The correct temperature and water will spur them to start the physical and chemical reactions needed. Sprouts grown in the dark will force the seed to put out stronger roots and not grow tall with a leafy top. If grown in too little light the sprout will grow leggy, or tall and thin. Mature sprouts will green up in a few hours. Put them out on a table in a sunny room after breakfast and they will be green enough to eat by lunchtime.

If, however, you are growing your sprouts in a dark basement, utility closet, or other place that does not get sufficient daylight, you may need to get artificial lighting for them. The lighting purchase need not be expensive or expansive. A grow light bought from the local hardware store or nursery will suffice. Remember, every additional purchase you make for your sprouts as you grow them increases the overall cost of the sprout harvest. Because they are happy to get green for you with a little bit of light, there is no need to make a large investment.

FERTILIZER AND GOOD NUTRITION

Everything a seed needs to become a sprout is right there in the seed. The seed provides all the nutrition the new plant needs to start its growth process. As it grows into a mature plant, it will need to pull additional nutrients in through its root system. We can enhance the nutrient content of the tiny sprout by using a fertilizer.

Our bodies can synthesize the proteins that they need as long as we provide them with the essential amino acids from our food. These amino acids are then combined, like building blocks, into proteins. We can make our own fats and carbohydrates, too, but we cannot make our own minerals.

Fertilizers add minerals to our sprouts, and when we eat the sprouts, we get the minerals. Minerals come from the earth and ocean water, so we need to have a good reliable source of minerals in our diets to make our bodies work properly. Fertilized sprouts are a great way to get these minerals.

Fertilizers are especially necessary when growing grasses and the larger sprouts like sunflower, buckwheat, and pea shoots. These sprouts take an extra few days to reach maturity, and using fertilizer for them is beneficial to their growth.

Choose an organic fertilizer for your sprouts. There are emulsified kelp fertilizers made from kelp found in the deep ocean waters. There are also fertilizers made from concentrating ocean water. You can use the fertilizer in the soaking of your seeds and after the rinsing of your sprouts. They can be used in soil methods or hydroponic methods. Use only organic fertilizers that are approved for vegetables.

Follow the directions from the manufacturer to dilute the concentrated fertilizer. Add some of the fertilizer to your soaking seeds. The soaking process is the most important part of sprouting because it is during the soaking that the seed turns from a dormant kernel of life into a living sprout. Mist the sprouts with a diluted mixture of the fertilizer and water after they have been rinsed and drained so that they can absorb the minerals. If you are growing grass or the shoots in soil, you can mist the sprouts near their roots while they are growing.

WATER

To become a sprout, a seed needs water. At the right temperature and given the right amount of rainwater, seeds can grow on pavement and asphalt. With the absorption of water, the seed starts its physical changes and chemical reactions and becomes a sprout. In our homes we can choose which water we will use to grow our sprouts.

Each household gets its drinking water in different ways. Some have wells, some rely on municipalities and their use of reservoirs and underground water sources, and some households purchase water in jugs from the store or have it delivered in larger amounts. Water we get at home through our faucets can be filtered or not.

You should always use the best water that is available to you. The source should give you fresh, clean water. If you always use tap water without a filter, that is fine. You can use tap water with a filter, too. You can have a whole-house filter or just the kitchen faucet filter. There are many different types of filtering systems available for household use. Just remember—sprouts do not need fancy filtering systems to grow. If someone tries to sell you a special filtering system just to grow your sprouts, he or she is trying to get you to spend money. There is no need to invest in new water systems for your home because you are sprouting. Use the water system that you have available to you and your family.

TEMPERATURE

Seeds want to sprout. That is their job and function in the world. They hold new life in them and under the right conditions they will sprout.

If you think about what goes on with Mother Nature outside, then you can imagine what a seed needs to become a sprout. Plants grow outside in the springtime when the temperatures begin to hover around 65°F (18°C). The soil warms from the winter cold, the sun shines for more hours, and there is more rain. A seed will sprout when the temperature is right and when there is enough moisture. Given these conditions, it will sprout even on cement or asphalt.

Similar conditions need to be met for indoor sprouting. Temperatures need to be near 65°F (18°C). Seeds can catch a draft if they are put in sprouters that are against an outside wall, even one that has insulation. Growth patterns will be disrupted by the draft. During the colder months, place your sprouter against an interior wall. If you have a very cold home or if you want to speed the process of germination and growth, try using a nursery seedling heat mat. These provide a very low level of heat and speed germination when placed under a sprouter. They can also dry out the sprouts, so you may need to rinse them more frequently throughout the day. Heat mats are not necessary beyond the germination stage.

SAFE FOOD–HANDLING PRACTICES

We have all read news stories about people getting sick from eating sprouts. *E. coli*, salmonella, listeria, and other bacteria all seem to be lurking in the background while we are growing and eating our sprouts at home. Remember, you cannot see, smell, or taste these bacteria. This is a very real concern but one that we can mitigate as home sprouters.

Two necessary steps need to be followed for safe food handling when sprouting at home before you even begin the sprouting process. First, it is very important to purchase quality seeds that have been tested for these bacteria by third-party independent laboratories. These are labs not owned by the farmer or the supplier. At the point of testing the seeds will be noted as bacteria-free.

Also, it is critical to wash your sprouters very carefully in warm sudsy water and then rinse them in hot water. Mason jars used for sprouting can be washed in the dishwasher. Some plastic sprouters can be washed in the dishwasher, usually on the upper rack, but it is always best to follow the manufacturer's guidelines. If you have the time and the space, dry your sprouters outside in the sunshine. Bacteria hate sunshine.

Wash your hands for 20 seconds with a mild soap in hot sudsy water before you touch your seeds/sprouts either for rinsing or for eating. We humans are capable of picking up bacteria along the way during our day. Because we do not want to ingest any of that, it is a good idea to wash our hands before touching our food, and that includes the seeds and the sprouts as they are growing.

You should use clean fresh water not only when soaking the seeds but also throughout the sprouting process. The source of the water is very important. Most municipalities treat water before it gets to the home. Well water users can have their wells tested by the local health department.

Some people may want to sanitize their seeds. If you are a commercial grower this is a must and you need to follow the guidelines put forth by the Food and Drug Administration (FDA) to ensure the safety of your product. For the home sprouter this is a choice.

The FDA recommends sanitizing your seeds as part of their outlined safe food-handling procedures. You can do this easily by mixing 1 ounce (30 ml) of regular household bleach with 10 ounces (300 ml) of water. Soak the seeds in this mixture for 5 minutes, then rinse them three times with fresh water. After this procedure you can begin the process of sprouting. This is only a recommendation. You can also use $1/2$ teaspoon of 35% hydrogen

Emphasis for the home sprouter should be on creating conditions that do not allow mold or bacteria to grow. Plastic tray sprouters that stack one on top of another and drain from one to the other can become the perfect environment for growing bacteria. The water is poured into the top tray and that water trickles down to the middle tray or trays and finally to the bottom tray. As the water trickles down it freely allows bacteria to move from top to bottom. There is little air circulation. The warm plastic environment creates the perfect set of conditions for bacteria growth and mold.

The best way to safely use these stackable trays is to rinse each tray individually, allowing the water to drain out of the tray completely before restacking the sprouter. In this way, only fresh water touches the sprouts and by rinsing each tray individually air circulation is fostered. This method takes a little bit longer but is the safest way.

By following these guidelines sprouting at home can be a safe activity to be enjoyed for many years.

Be careful, too, of cross-contamination. Don't touch your sprouts or other vegetables when handling raw meat such as chicken, beef, pork, fish, or even eggs. Try to keep everything separate. It is also a good idea to wash and clean counters before going from one type of food preparation to another. Don't prepare your sprout salad with the same cutting board or utensils used for your meat preparation. Do not drink or otherwise consume the water that the sprouts are soaked in overnight, or the rinsing water. The soaking water contains by-products of the chemical reactions that started the germination process. It may also have bacteria in it, as may the rinsing water. You can recycle the water on your houseplants or outdoor garden, but it is not for human consumption.

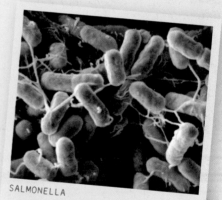

SALMONELLA

E. COLI

peroxide to 16 ounces (470 ml) of water. Soak for 5 minutes, then rinse well. Remember, the FDA recommendation is for chlorination with regular household bleach. Test after test shows that chlorine really works; other additives, such as hydrogen peroxide and grapefruit seed extract, are not mentioned by the FDA.

TROUBLE-SHOOTING

Sometimes our sprouts do not feel well because they're attacked by unseen foes. Once the problem is identified we can take steps to help them overcome their ailments and reduce the chance of recurrence.

MOLD, MILDEW, AND CILIA HAIRS

What is that white stuff growing on my new sprouts? Is it mold? Is it mildew? Something else? Not all mold is mold or mildew; sometimes it's something else. When sprouts are thirsty they put out tiny little microscopic cells called cilia hairs. Cilia hairs are very small cells but we can see them because the roots of the sprouts put out so many. They are tiny enough to get moisture from the atmosphere. This means that the sprouts are thirsty.

If it is mold or mildew, then there will be a horribly disgusting odor associated with it. If it is mold or mildew, then it will have a slight gray or blue-gray tint to it and it will be slimy to the touch; the sliminess will not rinse away.

If it is not mold but cilia hairs, there is no disgusting odor associated with it. It is not slimy to the touch and it does rinse away only to come back several hours later. If it is not mold, it is white in color, like a nice cloud that your sprouts can get moisture from.

What to do? Rinse the sprouts for a longer period of time. You are Mother Nature to them; they can only get their moisture if you provide it for them. So provide them with the water that they need. If you are rinsing your sprouts under the faucet, then sing a nice little song to them for a few minutes. "I love my sprouts, and they love me" is a nice tune. If you are soaking them, then go ahead and brush your teeth or comb your hair. Give them some time with the water. Drain away the excess water when they are done so that you have only wet sprouts and no standing water. You may want to rinse an extra time during the day, but really, just give them more time with the water and that should take care of the cilia hair cloud.

Mold is a product of moisture and temperature. To prevent mold from growing you need to lower the temperature of your growing sprouts. Sprouts create heat as they grow, and that heat, coupled with moisture, will promote the growth of mold. To lower the temperature you can put your growing sprouts in the refrigerator for several hours each day or overnight. Or you can point a fan directly at your sprouts. This will lower the temperature and also increase air circulation, two things that mold does not like at all. You can also use fewer seeds in the sprouter, particularly during the warmer months.

Remember not to eat sprouts that you think may have mold or mildew on them. Discard those sprouts, sterilize your sprouter, and start over again. It happens to all of us—new sprouters and veterans alike. We all have the capability to grow mold and mildew. Move on to the next batch of sprouts.

MOLD ON WHEATGRASS

COMMON GNAT

FRUIT FLY

FRUIT FLIES AND GNATS

Do you ever get those tiny, annoying, buzzing bugs around your growing sprouts or wheatgrass? Swatting the air around the trays only seems to make them irritated enough to rise as a cloud before settling back down to roam around your tasty new vegetable forest like they were on a relaxing camping trip. Home sprouters everywhere have at one time or another experienced the tiny flying bug problem.

Although many people identify these creatures correctly as fruit flies, they are often referred to as gnats. Both gnats and fruits flies are so tiny that it is difficult to tell them apart, but there are differences between the two bugs.

They are both classified as from the animal kingdom, phylum *Arthropoda*, class Insecta order, *Diptera*. The fruit fly belongs to the family *Drosophilidae*, species *Drosophila melanogaster*. The gnat belongs to other families such as *Mycetophilidae*, *Anisopodidae*, and *Sciaridae*, and they have different species, too.

Gnats can be found outdoors and not in our homes. They tend to feed on blood, but there are gnats that feed on plant materials outside. What we find in our kitchens are fruit flies. They come into our homes on and in the fruits and vegetables that we bring inside. The female fruit fly lays her eggs inside an apple, for example, after puncturing its skin. The eggs and the larvae are invited into our kitchens. Fruits flies do not come on the sprouting seeds. Once they become adult fruit flies they drift over to our sprouts, attracted to the location by the moist, warm atmosphere that we have cultivated to grow them. And they fly around and make us miserable.

What can you do about this problem? You can wash the fruits and veggies that you bring indoors, refrigerate them, and do not let them sit on the counter. Reduce the temperature of your growing sprouts. Fruit flies like warm, moist places with little or no air circulation. Put your trays or jars of growing sprouts into the fridge for a few hours each day or overnight to cool down the sprouts. You can also point a fan directly at the growing sprouts. The fan will move the air around and that will upset the flies and they will not settle on the sprouts. Using a little less seed to have a thinner sprout garden also helps with air circulation. Keep mature sprouts refrigerated so that the insects do not have a place to gather.

STORING MATURE SPROUTS

Has this happened to you? Everything is going along fine with your sprouting. You have successfully soaked those seeds and they are now on day 3 of sprouting. Actual progress in the growing cycle can be seen as evidenced by the root and a little bit of a sprout coming through the seed casing. Rinsing two times each day and keeping the growing sprouts at the correct temperature has allowed all of this to happen, and in a few days' time you will be ready to eat this harvest.

But then you are called away and have to leave home and leave the sprouts. Or you neglected in your planning to take into account that you have travel plans for the weekend. Or you get sick or someone else in your household gets sick and everything is topsy-turvy. What to do with those growing sprouts?

Rinse them, drain them well so they are not damp and there is no standing water, cover them in an airtight container, and put them into the refrigerator. They will think it turned to winter and will go to sleep for a little while. Their growth will continue, however slowly, just like grass continues to grow at a snail's pace through the winter months. When you are ready, take them out of the refrigerator, give them a nice bath or a little soaking time, drain them well, and resume the sprouting process. Once they get acclimated to being warmed up again, they will begin to grow, and in a few days' time you will get your harvest of mature sprouts.

Sprouts stored this way will last for about a week. If they are stored longer than a week, it may be best to start the process all over again.

The fresh mature sprouts can be eaten and enjoyed. But let's say you have a large batch of sprouts and you cannot eat them all at once. You can store mature sprouts in the refrigerator. Give them a nice rinsing and drain them well so they are not damp and there is no standing water, cover them in an airtight container, and put them in the refrigerator. The lower temperature of the refrigerator will keep them crisp and ready to eat. If they are going to stay in the fridge for several days, you may want to give them a nice rinsing and draining during that time because they can get dehydrated and need some water to feel rejuvenated again. Don't forget about them, and remember to enjoy them.

People who do large batch sprouting often use this method to keep the mature sprouts ready to eat. Juicers who grow large quantities of sprouts or grasses can use these ideas to make sure they have enough greens to juice throughout the week.

If you have a large quantity of either wheatgrass or barley grass, you can juice the grass and then store the juice. Freeze the juice in ice cube trays so that it can be thawed quickly. This method, although not as ideal as drinking the freshly juiced grass, can be used to keep the nutritious green elixir for future use.

Just remember the sprouts are there, waiting for you.

REMOVING HULLS

Hulls are the seed casings that no longer hold in the seed. They have been broken open by the emerging sprout and are no longer necessary. Once opened fully and discarded by the seed, hulls can get mixed up with the mature sprouts. Their flavor is often bitter in contrast to the sweet natural taste of the sprout. You can remove the hulls before eating the mature sprouts.

Take the mature sprouts that you want to eat, put them in a bowl of fresh water, and vigorously swish them around. This will allow the hulls to float to the top. Once the hulls are floating they are easily removed. For the leafy types of sprouts you can take a handful and place them directly under strong running water from the tap. Let the water flow onto the sprouts and the hulls will fall off.

Some people have great success using a salad spinner. Put the sprouts inside of the spinner and fill it with water. Let the hulls float off before draining out the water. Once you have only sprouts in the mesh part, start the spinning. More hulls should spin out.

Hulls are insoluble fiber and can be eaten. They will go right through you, although the larger hulls on sunflower and buckwheat cannot be easily digested. For these sprouts, if the hulls do not come off by themselves it may be necessary to remove them manually, hull by hull, off of the mature sprout. Do this to music or make it into a meditation and you will find that the work goes quickly and easily. In the end, you will have a delicious serving of fresh green sprouts.

TO REMOVE HULLS, PLACE THE MATURE SPROUTS IN FRESH WATER AND VIGOROUSLY SWISH THEM AROUND.

SPROUTING ECONOMICS

There are many places where you can buy mature sprouts. Several companies market their wares to health food stores and groceries stores. These sprouts come in clamshell packaging and can be found in the vegetable aisle. They are frequently labeled organic and are typically the most popular variety of sprouts; the most common are alfalfa, mung bean, clover, radish, and broccoli. Health food stores or juice bars also carry mature grass for sale so that you can juice at home. Farmers' markets have vendors that supply fresh sprouts and these can be of the more unusual varieties, such as onion, garlic, sunflower, and snow pea shoots, offered along with other staples of the farm.

Purchasing small amounts of mature sprouts in stores can get expensive if you eat sprouts every day. If you are trying to eat more sprouts and have some at lunch and some at dinner,

you may find yourself eating one container per day. Multiply that by the number of other people in your household and those few dollars per container can add up to an expensive food habit, and one that may keep growing.

Shots of wheatgrass juice of about 1 or 2 ounces (30 or 60 ml) each can cost several dollars. In major metropolitan areas, single shots of the green elixir can get into almost double-digit amounts. Buying flats of fresh grown wheatgrass to juice at home is very expensive, especially when you need a volume amount of grass to get a small amount of juice, and you need to add delivery cost charges. A single flat typically yields only about 8 ounces (235 ml) of juice—a two- or three-day supply for basic health maintenance. You may need a few flats per person to get through the week.

Investing in a few sprouting tools to add to your kitchen can save money in the long run. A sprouter, good-quality seeds, and water are all you need to get those tasty new vegetables into your home and diet. Once you find the sprouting method that works the best for you and your needs, your sprouter will last you for many years to come.

Note that ¼ cup (25 g) of a tiny seed like alfalfa or broccoli will yield about 8 cups (400 g) of mature sprouts. One cup (50 g) of leafy green sprouts eaten per day is enough to help make a change in your body. Two cups (200 g) of hard wheat seed can grow into an entire flat of grass to yield several ounces of juice. Half a cup (95 g) of dry beans or legumes can turn into more than a full cup (50 g) of sprouts and more than one serving of sprouted beans and grains for a meal.

There is the convenience factor of buying those already grown sprouts at the store. You see them while you are buying your other vegetables, put the container in your cart, and when you get home place them in the refrigerator until you are ready to eat them. How convenient is it to grow your own? Soak the seeds overnight, pour them into the sprouter, then rinse and drain two times each day. In several days, you have mature sprouts ready to eat after just a few minutes of your time. Thus, consider the economy of sprouting your own:

THE SPROUTER WILL MORE THAN PAY FOR ITSELF OVER THE YEARS.

The price of the seeds per pound (454 g) is just a fraction of the cost of similar types of mature organic vegetables.

The time you spend on sprouting reaps the reward of eating your own homegrown sprouts.

The economics of running an efficient household all point to sprouting for yourself and your family.

PART II:
HOW TO SPROUT

CHAPTER 4:
BEANS AND LEGUMES

SPROUTED BEANS AND LEGUMES ARE YOUR BEST SOURCE FOR PROTEIN. THEY ARE QUICK TO SPROUT, RETAIN A GREAT CRUNCH, AND HAVE A MILD TASTE. SPROUTED BEANS AND LEGUMES CAN ALSO BE ADDED AT THE LAST MINUTE TO SOUPS AND STIR-FRIES WITHOUT TAKING AWAY THEIR NUTRITION. LENTILS, MARROWFAT GREEN PEAS, SWEET GREEN PEAS, MUNG, SOY, BLACK TURTLE, ADZUKI, AND GARBANZO BEANS ALL FALL INTO THIS CATEGORY.

The larger beans like soy, green pea, marrowfat peas, garbanzo, pinto, and kidney can cause stomach distress for some people. Steaming these, adding them to soups at the last minute, or using them in stir-fries is often helpful. The heat begins the digestion process and makes them easier on the stomach. If these continue to give you stomach distress, even after slightly cooking them, then do not eat them anymore and stick to lentils, mung beans, and adzuki beans, which are smaller and more easily digested.

Beans and legumes are a low-fat food. Like other vegetables, these sprouts have no cholesterol and are a low-sodium food. They do have carbohydrates, but these are the good carbs, the ones your body needs from unprocessed whole food sources. They are gluten-free and a great source of minerals and some vitamins. Sprouted beans and legumes also have a lot of fiber. Add 1 cup (100 g) of sprouted beans to your day at small intervals, a handful here and a handful there, and you have simply and easily added nutrients and fiber to your diet.

HOW TO SPROUT BEANS AND LEGUMES IN A HEMP SPROUTING BAG

7

1 Follow safe food-handling procedures by using clean water from a reliable source for soaking and sprouting; wash your hands before touching the seeds or sprouts.

2 Measure your beans or legumes and put them in a jar or bowl.

3 Fill the jar with cool water from the tap.

4 Soak the beans in the jar overnight, about 8 to 10 hours. You can soak them for up to 24 hours with a water change in the middle at 12 hours.

5 If you want to use fertilizer, add it to the soaking water. You can also put some fertilizer in a spray bottle and mist some on the beans as they grow.

6 Prepare the bag by pre-moistening it.

7 Pour the water and beans into the bag and let the water drain out.

8 Rinse the seeds with fresh water under the tap while they are in the bag. Let the water drain away.

9 Hang the bag so that the water can drip. Never put your bag flat on a surface like a counter or plate. Doing so will cause the hemp material to rot.

10 Approximately every 12 hours, at least two times each day, rinse and drain the beans in the bag by running it under the tap. Alternatively, you can put the bag into a bowl of water and let it sit in the water for a minute or so. Pick up the bag and let the water drain. Be consistent in your rinsing and draining; the sprouts will grow very nicely if you remember to give them their baths. Inconsistent watering habits can cause changes in growth patterns.

11 Hang the bag so that the water can drip.

12 You can give your seeds a little massage through the bag after each rinsing. This will help keep the roots from growing into the bag.

13 Beans are ready to eat In about one to two days. Start counting the days after the initial soak.

14 Remove the sprouted beans or lentils from the bag and enjoy.

HOW TO SPROUT BEANS AND LEGUMES IN AN EASY SPROUTER

1 Follow safe food-handling procedures by washing the Easy Sprouter in warm sudsy water and then rinsing in hot water; use clean water from a reliable source for soaking and sprouting. Wash your hands before touching the seeds or sprouts.

2 Measure your beans or legumes in the dome with graduated markings and pour them into the inner container, the smaller one that has openings in the bottom. Put the inner container into the solid outer container.

3 Fill the Easy Sprouter with cool water from the tap.

4 Soak the beans in the Easy Sprouter overnight, about 8 to 10 hours. You can soak them for up to 24 hours with a water change in the middle at 12 hours.

5 If you want to use fertilizer, add it to the soaking water. You can also put some fertilizer in a spray bottle and mist some on the beans as they grow.

6 Lift out the inner container and let the water drain. Empty the outer container of any standing water.

7 Put the inner container back into the outer container and fill the Easy Sprouter with fresh water.

8 Give the beans a minute or so and let them absorb the water and enjoy their bath. Water is not only necessary for the sprouting process, but it also rinses away bacteria. Lift out the inner container and let the water drain so that you are left with only wet beans in the Easy Sprouter and no standing water. Empty the outer container of any standing water.

9 Approximately every 12 hours, at least two times each day, rinse and drain the beans, making certain that there is no standing water left in the Easy Sprouter, only wet seeds or sprouts. Be consistent in your rinsing and draining; the sprouts will grow very nicely if you remember to give them their baths. Inconsistent watering habits can cause changes in growth patterns.

10 The Dual Container System in the Easy Sprouter allows for air circulation, which helps eliminate the chances of mold and mildew growth.

11 Beans are ready to eat in about one to two days. Start counting the days after the initial soak.

12 Remove the sprouted beans or legumes from the Easy Sprouter and enjoy.

HOW TO SPROUT BEANS AND LEGUMES IN A TRAY SPROUTER

5

1 Follow safe food-handling procedures by washing the sprouter in warm sudsy water and then rinsing in hot water; use clean water from a reliable source for soaking and sprouting. Wash your hands before touching the seeds or sprouts.

2 Measure your beans or legumes and put them into a jar or bowl of cool water from the tap.

3 Soak the beans in the jar or bowl overnight, about 8 to 10 hours. You can soak them for up to 24 hours with a water change in the middle at 12 hours.

4 If you want to use fertilizer, add it to the soaking water. You can also put some fertilizer in a spray bottle and mist some on the beans as they grow.

5 Pour the seeds into the tray over a sink and let the water drain out. Rinse the seeds in the tray with fresh water and let that water drain. There should be only wet seeds or sprouts in the tray and no standing water.

6 Some tray sprouters come with solid trays for underneath the tray and lids to cover the tray. Some tray sprouters stack trays on top of each other and the top tray has a cover. These methods are used to create a greenhouse effect so that the beans or lentils do not dry out during the sprouting process. Assemble and cover your sprouter according to the manufacturer's guidelines.

7 Approximately every 12 hours, at least two times each day, rinse and drain the beans, making certain that there is no standing water left in the tray, only wet seeds or sprouts. Be consistent in your rinsing and draining; the sprouts will grow very nicely if you remember to give them their baths. Inconsistent watering habits can cause changes in growth patterns. Do not rush; give them some time with the water running over them.

8 Beans are ready to eat in about one to two days. Start counting the days after the initial soak.

9 Remove the sprouted beans from the tray and enjoy.

HOW TO SPROUT BEANS AND LEGUMES IN A TERRA-COTTA CLAY SPROUTER

5

1 Follow safe food-handling procedures by washing the sprouter in warm sudsy water and then rinsing in hot water; use clean water from a reliable source for soaking and sprouting. Wash your hands before touching the seeds or sprouts. Make certain the holes in the tray are cleared and not clogged. You can use a needle or paper clip end to poke out any debris left over from a previous sprouting event.

2 Measure your beans or legumes and put them into a jar or bowl of cool water from the tap.

3 Soak the beans in the jar or bowl overnight, about 8 to 10 hours. You can soak them for up to 24 hours with a water change in the middle at 12 hours.

4 If you want to use fertilizer, add it to the soaking water. You can also put some fertilizer in a spray bottle and mist some on the beans and lentils as they grow.

5 Prepare the terra-cotta clay sprouter for sprouting by presoaking the tray in water for about 5 minutes, or you can let it sit in water for up to 15 minutes. The tray will absorb some of the water because it is porous.

6 Remove the tray from the water and pour the soaking beans into the tray over a sink. Let the water drain out. This may take several minutes because the clay will absorb some of the water. Rinse the seeds in the tray with fresh water and let that water drain. There should be only wet seeds or sprouts in the tray and no standing water.

7 Assemble your sprouter according to the manufacturer's directions.

8 Approximately every 12 hours, at least two times each day, rinse and drain the beans, making certain that there is no standing water left in the tray, only wet seeds or sprouts. Be consistent in your rinsing and draining; the sprouts will grow very nicely if you remember to give them their baths. Inconsistent watering habits can cause changes in growth patterns.

9 Beans are ready to eat in about one to two days. Start counting the days after the initial soak.

10 Remove the sprouted beans from the clay tray and enjoy.

HOW TO SPROUT BEANS AND LEGUMES IN AN EASYGREEN AUTOMATIC SPROUTER

1 Assemble the EasyGreen Automatic Sprouter according to the manufacturer's setup directions. The timer supplied can mist and oxygenate in time increments of approximately 15 minutes.

2 Follow safe food-handling procedures by washing the trays or cartridges in warm sudsy water and then rinsing in hot water; use clean water from a reliable source to fill the water reservoir. Wash your hands before touching the seeds or sprouts. Make certain the holes in the trays or cartridges are cleared and not clogged. You can use a needle or paper clip end to poke out any debris left over from a previous sprouting event.

3 Notice that the water reservoir is in the back of the machine and the sprouts are in the cavity in the front of the machine. The wastewater drains away after the misting so that only fresh water touches the sprouts and not recycled water. Some automatic sprouters have the water reservoir below the seeds and the water is recirculated from the bottom to the top by the pump. Reused and recirculated water in a warm plastic environment is the perfect place to grow bacteria. The EasyGreen Automatic Sprouter allows only fresh water to touch the sprouts. Using an electric automatic sprouter eliminates the need to presoak the seeds.

4 If you want to use fertilizer, add it to the reservoir water.

5 Wet the cartridges with water so that the seeds "stick" and do not jump around from static electricity. Sprinkle an even layer of beans or legumes in a cartridge and shake the cartridge gently from side to side to even out the layer.

6 Put the cartridge in the cavity of the machine. Put in the other empty cartridges as well, so the bean-filled cartridge is on the right side of the cavity and the empty ones are to the left. Move the seed cartridges daily one cartridge width to the left and place the new seeded cartridges to the far right. This way, you have enough sprouts to eat every day.

7 Beans are ready to eat in about one to two days. Replenish the empty cartridges with new beans to continue the sprouting cycle.

8 Remove the sprouted beans from the cartridges and enjoy.

HOW TO SPROUT ADZUKI AND MUNG BEANS

Do you enjoy the bean sprouts that you eat at a Chinese restaurant or find at a salad bar? You can grow these yourself at home. There are two things you need to remember to accomplish this task: the seeds need to be grown in the dark and under pressure. When you grow the beans in the dark, they stay white, crispy, and sweet. When light gets to the sprouts it makes them tougher due to the process of photosynthesis, which causes cellulose development and chlorophyll. By growing them under pressure you cause them to grow fatter and they become very crunchy.

You can be creative in your choice of container and weight system. A tray sprouter will work fine if you can fashion a smaller lid that will fit inside the walls of the tray and allow weight, such as a brick or some stones, to be put on top. Another system that may work is a bucket nestled inside another bucket. Stainless steel or food-grade plastic buckets work best. Do not use galvanized steel. You can use a dark plastic trash bag to wrap around your do-it-yourself sprouter to ensure the light stays out.

Be consistent in your rinsing and draining by doing this task two times each day. The sprouts will grow very nicely if you remember to give them their baths. Inconsistent watering habits can cause changes in growth patterns.

These sprouts are ready to eat in four to five days when they are plump and juicy. Enjoy!

CHAPTER 5:
GRAINS

SPROUTED GRAINS ARE A GREAT SOURCE OF FIBER AND GOOD CARBOHYDRATES, THE ONES YOUR BODY NEEDS FROM UNPROCESSED WHOLE FOOD SOURCES. THIS IS ABOUT THE MOST UNPROCESSED SOURCE YOU CAN ACHIEVE. GRAINS ARE VERY LOW IN SATURATED FAT AND SODIUM. LIKE OTHER VEGETABLES, THEY HAVE NO CHOLESTEROL. THEY ARE QUICK TO SPROUT, OFFER A CHEWY EXPERIENCE, AND ARE MILD IN TASTE. EASILY DIGESTED, SPROUTED GRAINS CAN ALSO BE ADDED AT THE LAST MINUTE TO SOUPS AND STIR-FRIES. AFTER SPROUTING, THEY CAN BE DEHYDRATED AND BECOME CRUNCHY AGAIN.

RINSING THEM TWO TIMES EACH DAY HELPS KEEP BACTERIA FROM GROWING AND ALLOWS AIR CIRCULATION. GRAINS DO NOT TAKE LONG TO SPROUT TO MATURITY, ABOUT ONE TO TWO DAYS.

HOW TO SPROUT GRAINS IN A MASON JAR USING A STAINLESS STEEL SCREEN OR PLASTIC SPROUTING LID

Grains sprout quickly and easily. They can add a sweet taste to any dish, along with plenty of fiber and some proteins.

1 Follow safe food-handling procedures by washing the jar and screen or lid in warm sudsy water and then rinsing in hot water; use clean water from a reliable source for soaking and sprouting. Wash your hands before touching the seeds or sprouts.

2 Measure your grains and put them in the jar.

3 Fill the jar with cool water from the tap.

4 Soak the grains in the jar overnight, about 8 to 10 hours. You can soak most grains for up to 24 hours with a water change in the middle at 12 hours.

5 If you want to use fertilizer, add it to the soaking water. You can also put some fertilizer in a spray bottle and mist some on the grains as they grow.

6 Screw the screen and rim or plastic lid onto the mason jar. Pour out the water so that you are left with only wet grains in the jar and no standing water.

7 Fill the jar with fresh water. Give the grains a minute or so and let them absorb the water and enjoy their bath. Pour out the water so that you are left with only wet grains in the jar and no standing water. Water is not only necessary for the sprouting process, but it also rinses away bacteria.

8 Place the jar upside down at an angle with the screen or lid on the bottom to allow the water to fully drain out. This helps cut down on bacteria growing in any standing water.

9 Approximately every 12 hours, at least two times each day, rinse and drain the grains, making certain that there is no standing water left in the jar, only wet seeds or sprouts.

Be consistent in your rinsing and draining; the sprouts will grow very nicely if you remember to give them their baths. Inconsistent watering habits can cause changes in growth patterns.

10 Grains are ready to eat in about one to two days. Start counting the days after the initial soak.

11 Remove the sprouted grains from the jar and enjoy.

HOW TO SPROUT GRAINS IN A HEMP SPROUTING BAG

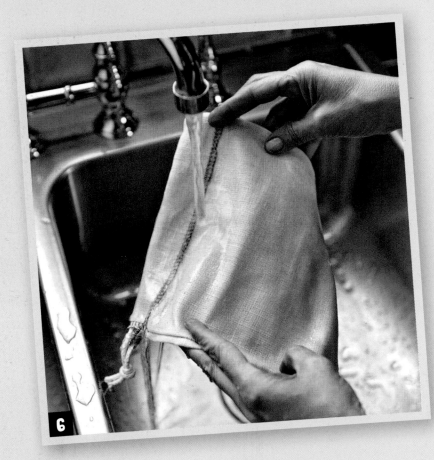

1 Follow safe food-handling procedures by using clean water from a reliable source for soaking and sprouting; wash your hands before touching the seeds or sprouts.

2 Measure your grains and put them in a jar or bowl.

3 Fill the jar with cool water from the tap.

4 Soak the grains in the jar overnight, about 8 to 10 hours. You can soak most grains for up to 24 hours with a water change in the middle at 12 hours.

5 If you want to use fertilizer, add it to the soaking water. You can also put some fertilizer in a spray bottle and mist some on the grains as they grow.

6 Prepare the bag by pre-moistening it.

7 Pour the water and grains into the bag and let the water drain out.

8 Rinse the seeds with fresh water under the tap while they are in the bag. Let the water drain away.

9 Hang the bag so that the water can drip. Never put your bag flat on a surface like a counter or plate. Doing so will cause the hemp material to rot.

10 Approximately every 12 hours, at least two times each day, rinse and drain the grains in the bag by running it under the tap. Alternatively, you can put the bag into a bowl of water and let it sit in the water for a minute or so. Pick up the bag and let the water drain.

Be consistent in your rinsing and draining; the sprouts will grow very nicely if you remember to give them their baths. Inconsistent watering habits can cause changes in growth patterns.

11 Hang the bag so that the water can drip.

12 You can give your seeds a little massage through the bag after each rinsing. This will help keep the roots from growing into the bag.

13 Grains are ready to eat in about one to two days. Start counting the days after the initial soak.

14 Remove the sprouted grains from the bag and enjoy.

8

HOW TO SPROUT GRAINS IN AN EASY SPROUTER

1 Follow safe food-handling procedures by washing the Easy Sprouter in warm sudsy water and then rinsing in hot water; use clean water from a reliable source for soaking and sprouting. Wash your hands before touching the seeds or sprouts.

2 Measure your grains in the dome with graduated markings and pour them into the inner container, the smaller one that has openings in the bottom. Put the inner container into the solid outer container.

3 Fill the Easy Sprouter with cool water from the tap.

4 Soak the grains in the Easy Sprouter overnight, about 8 to 10 hours. You can soak most grains for up to 24 hours with a water change in the middle at 12 hours.

5 If you want to use fertilizer, add it to the soaking water. You can also put some fertilizer in a spray bottle and mist some on the grains as they grow.

6 Lift out the inner container and let the water drain. Empty the outer container of any standing water.

7 Put the inner container back into the outer container and fill the Easy Sprouter with fresh water.

8 Give the grains a minute or so and let them absorb the water and enjoy their bath. Lift out the inner container and let the water drain so that you are left with only wet grains in the Easy Sprouter and no standing water. Empty the outer container of any standing water.

9 Approximately every 12 hours, at least two times each day, rinse and drain the grains, making certain that there is no standing water left in the Easy Sprouter, only wet grains or sprouts. Be consistent in your rinsing and draining; the sprouts will grow very nicely if you remember to give them their baths. Inconsistent watering habits can cause changes in growth patterns.

The Dual Container System in the Easy Sprouter allows for air circulation, which helps eliminate the chances of mold and mildew growth.

10 Grains are ready to eat in about one to two days. Start counting the days after the initial soak.

11 Remove the sprouted grains from the Easy Sprouter and enjoy.

HOW TO SPROUT GRAINS IN A TRAY SPROUTER

1 Follow safe food-handling procedures by washing the sprouter in warm sudsy water and then rinsing in hot water; use clean water from a reliable source for soaking and sprouting. Wash your hands before touching the seeds or sprouts.

2 Measure your grains and put them into a jar or bowl of cool water from the tap.

3 Soak the grains in the jar or bowl overnight, about 8 to 10 hours. You can soak them for up to 24 hours with a water change in the middle at 12 hours.

4 If you want to use fertilizer, add it to the soaking water. You can also put some fertilizer in a spray bottle and mist some on the grains as they grow.

5 Pour the seeds into the tray over a sink and let the water drain out. Rinse the seeds in the tray with fresh water and let that water drain. There should be only wet seeds or sprouts in the tray and no standing water.

5

6

6 Some tray sprouters come with solid trays for underneath the tray and lids to cover the tray. Some tray sprouters stack trays on top of each other and the top tray has a cover. These methods are used to create a greenhouse effect so that the grains do not dry out during the sprouting process. Assemble and cover your sprouter according to the manufacturer's guidelines.

7 Approximately every 12 hours, at least two times each day, rinse and drain the grains, making certain that there is no standing water left in the tray, only wet seeds or sprouts. Be consistent in your rinsing and draining; the sprouts will grow very nicely if you remember to give them their baths. Inconsistent watering habits can cause changes in growth patterns. Do not rush; give them some time with the water running over them.

8 Grains are ready to eat in about one to two days. Start counting the days after the initial soak.

9 Remove the sprouted grains from the tray and enjoy.

HOW TO SPROUT GRAINS IN A TERRA-COTTA CLAY SPROUTER

1 Follow safe food-handling procedures by washing the sprouter in warm sudsy water and then rinsing in hot water; use clean water from a reliable source for soaking and sprouting. Wash your hands before touching the seeds or sprouts. Make certain the holes in the tray are cleared and not clogged. You can use a needle or paper clip end to poke out any debris left over from a previous sprouting event.

2 Measure your grains and put them into a jar or bowl of cool water from the tap.

3 Soak the grains in the jar or bowl overnight, about 8 to 10 hours. You can soak them for up to 24 hours with a water change in the middle at 12 hours.

4 If you want to use fertilizer, add it to the soaking water. You can also put some fertilizer in a spray bottle and mist some on the grains as they grow.

5 Prepare the terra-cotta clay sprouter by presoaking the tray in water for about 5 minutes, or you can let it sit in water for up to 15 minutes. The tray will absorb some of the water because it is porous.

6 Remove the tray from the water and pour the soaking grains into the tray over a sink. Let the water drain out. This may take several minutes because the clay will absorb some of the water. Rinse the seeds in the tray with fresh water and let that water drain. There should be only wet seeds or sprouts in the tray and no standing water.

7 Assemble your sprouter according to the manufacturer's directions.

8 Approximately every 12 hours, at least two times each day, rinse and drain the grains, making certain that there is no standing water left in the tray, only wet seeds or sprouts. Be consistent in your rinsing and draining; the sprouts will grow very nicely if you remember to give them their baths. Inconsistent watering habits can cause changes in growth patterns.

9 Grains are ready to eat in about one to two days. Start counting the days after the initial soak.

10 Remove the sprouted grains from the tray and enjoy.

HOW TO SPROUT GRAINS IN AN EASYGREEN AUTOMATIC SPROUTER

1 Assemble the EasyGreen Automatic Sprouter according to the manufacturer's setup directions. The timer supplied can mist and oxygenate in time increments of approximately 15 minutes.

2 Follow safe food-handling procedures by washing the trays or cartridges in warm sudsy water and then rinsing in hot water; use clean water from a reliable source to fill the water reservoir. Wash your hands before touching the seeds or sprouts. Make certain the holes in the trays or cartridges are cleared and not clogged. You can use a needle or paper clip end to poke out any debris left over from a previous sprouting event.

3 If you want to use fertilizer, add it to the reservoir.

4 Using an electric automatic sprouter eliminates the need to presoak the seeds. Wet the cartridges with water so that the seeds "stick" and do not jump around from static electricity. Sprinkle an even layer of grains in a cartridge and shake the cartridge gently from side to side to even out the layer.

5 Put the cartridge in the cavity of the machine. Put in the other empty cartridges as well, so the grain-filled cartridge is on the right side of the cavity and the empty ones are to the left.

Move the seed cartridges daily one cartridge width to the left and place the new seeded cartridges to the far right. This way, you have enough sprouts to eat every day.

6 Grains are ready to eat in about one to two days. Replenish the empty cartridges with new grains to continue the sprouting cycle.

7 Remove the sprouted grains from the trays and enjoy.

CHAPTER 6:
LEAFY GREEN SEEDS

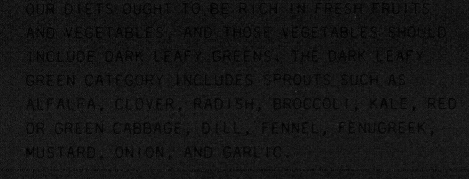

... OUR DIETS OUGHT TO BE RICH IN FRESH FRUITS AND VEGETABLES, AND THOSE VEGETABLES SHOULD INCLUDE DARK LEAFY GREENS. THE DARK LEAFY GREEN CATEGORY INCLUDES SPROUTS SUCH AS ALFALFA, CLOVER, RADISH, BROCCOLI, KALE, RED OR GREEN CABBAGE, DILL, FENNEL, FENUGREEK, MUSTARD, ONION, AND GARLIC.

These small seeds sprout into a powerhouse of readily accessible nutrition. When sprouted, they are a great gluten-free source of vitamins, fiber, minerals, and chlorophyll—the stuff that makes them green. Some are mild in taste and others are hot or spicy. Most of these seeds take about a week to sprout while some—onion, garlic, dill, and fennel—need a little bit longer, but they are well worth the wait.

Sprouted leafy greens are crunchy and easy to digest. They can be eaten as is or in salads or raw sprouted soups, and they are great for juicing because of their high water content.

They are a no-fat, low-sodium, and no-cholesterol food. The carbohydrates they offer are a source of fiber. This is the good type of carbs, the ones your body needs from unprocessed whole food sources.

Try to eat 1 cup (50 g) of leafy green sprouts per day. When you measure it out, it is not a lot of food but can be enough to make a change. The American Cancer Society and other organizations recommend 2 ½ cups (375 g) of fruits and veggies each day to help prevent certain types of cancers and reduce the risk of heart disease and diabetes. One-third of a cup (17 g) of leafy green sprouts at each meal makes the amount consumed seem even less.

MICROGREENS

Microgreens are sprouts that have been grown past the sprouting stage until the first true leaf appears. They are larger than sprouts and have an appearance closer to a plant with a fuller leaf and stem. Microgreens are grown in soil and take more time from seed to harvest.

Although they do not have the same amount of nutrition as sprouts do, they have more chlorophyll—the stuff that makes leaves green. Chlorophyll is what nutritionists want us to consume for healthy diets when they counsel us to eat more dark leafy green vegetables. Sprouts and microgreens both meet that requirement, and because microgreens are larger in size than sprouts, they also have more fiber.

It takes about twenty-five days to get a seed to a microgreen. Not all seeds do well as microgreens, but any of the ones in the Brassica family, such as broccoli, mizuna, mustard greens, tatsoi, beet, radish, kale, and cabbage, make nice ones and are often ready to eat in less than 25 days. So, too, do cress, basil, and arugula. They often taste like their mature counterparts—kale microgreens taste like mature kale. You can mix the seeds before planting so that they grow in a group with different flavors.

Sprinkle seeds on soil. Keep the soil moist with good drainage at a warm temperature for seed germination. There's no need for light during the growth stage. Soon you will see the sprout come up above the soil line. Avoid the temptation to eat the sprout! The sprout will get bigger and taller. After about twenty-five days it will be ready to harvest. You can taste the microgreen as it grows and determine which day you like best for harvesting. Just do so before the first true leaf arrives for a sweet-tasting, crunchy green. Snip the green above the soil line for harvesting, then rinse and enjoy! Do not eat any of the soil; you don't want that inside your body. You only want the green.

HOW TO SPROUT LEAFY GREENS

Sprouted leafy greens mature somewhere between five and seven days, shorter in the warmer temperatures and longer in the cooler temperatures. The exceptions to this are dill, fennel, onion, and garlic, which can take almost two weeks to reach maturity. You can do a taste test to see which day you prefer to harvest them, but don't let them go too long because their nutritional value declines as they get older.

Before harvesting these sprouts they need to "green up." By exposing them to any ordinary daylight that comes into a room, the process of photosynthesis will begin to develop chlorophyll. It only takes a few hours, for example from breakfast to lunch, to turn them green.

Leafy green sprouts grow nicely in jars and tray sprouters that allow them room to grow. Hemp bags don't have the space that leafy greens need and aren't a good option.

HOW TO SPROUT LEAFY GREENS IN A MASON JAR USING A STAINLESS STEEL SCREEN OR PLASTIC SPROUTING LID

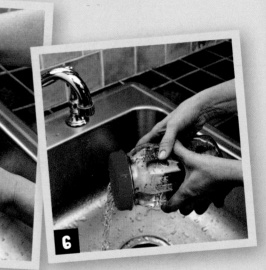

1 Follow safe food-handling procedures by washing the jar and screen or lid in warm sudsy water and then rinsing in hot water; use clean water from a reliable source for soaking and sprouting. Wash your hands before touching the seeds or sprouts.

2 Measure your seeds and put them in the jar.

3 Fill the jar with cool water from the tap.

4 Soak the seeds in the jar overnight, about 8 to 10 hours. You can soak them for up to 24 hours with a water change in the middle at 12 hours.

5 If you want to use fertilizer, add it to the soaking water. You can also put some fertilizer in a spray bottle and mist some on the sprouts as they grow.

6 Screw the screen and rim or plastic lid onto the mason jar. Pour out the water so that you are left with only wet seeds in the jar and no standing water.

7 Fill the jar with fresh water. Give the seeds or sprouts a minute or so and let them absorb the water and enjoy their bath. Pour out the water so that you are left with only wet seeds or sprouts in the jar and no standing water. Water is not only necessary for the sprouting process, but it also rinses away bacteria.

8 Place the jar upside down at an angle with the screen or lid on the bottom to allow the water to fully drain out. This helps cut down on bacteria growing in any standing water.

9 Approximately every 12 hours, at least two times each day, rinse and drain the seeds or sprouts, making certain that there is no standing water left in the jar, only wet seeds or sprouts.

Be consistent in your rinsing and draining; the sprouts will grow very nicely if you remember to give them their baths. Inconsistent watering habits can cause changes in growth patterns.

10 Leafy green sprouts are ready to eat in about five to seven days. Start counting the days after the initial soak. Dill and fennel take eight to ten days; garlic and onion can take almost two weeks.

11 Before the harvest, green up the sprouts by exposing them to ordinary daylight for a few hours.

12 Remove the sprouts from the jar and enjoy.

HOW TO SPROUT LEAFY GREENS IN AN EASY SPROUTER

1 Follow safe food-handling procedures by washing the Easy Sprouter in warm sudsy water and then rinsing in hot water; use clean water from a reliable source for soaking and sprouting. Wash your hands before touching the seeds or sprouts.

2 Measure your seeds in the dome with graduated markings and pour them into the inner container, the smaller one that has openings in the bottom. Put the inner container into the solid outer container.

3 Fill the Easy Sprouter with cool water from the tap.

4 Soak the seeds in the Easy Sprouter overnight, about 8 to 10 hours. You can soak them for up to 24 hours with a water change in the middle at 12 hours.

5 If you want to use fertilizer, add it to the soaking water. You can also put some fertilizer in a spray bottle and mist some on the sprouts as they grow.

6 Lift out the inner container and let the water drain. Empty the outer container of any standing water.

7 Put the inner container back into the outer container and fill the Easy Sprouter with fresh water.

8 Give the seeds or sprouts a minute or so and let them absorb the water and enjoy their bath. Water is not only necessary for the sprouting process, but it also rinses away bacteria. Lift out the inner container and let the water drain so that you are left with only wet seeds or sprouts in the Easy Sprouter and no standing water. Empty the outer container of any standing water.

9 Approximately every 12 hours, at least two times each day, rinse and drain the seeds or sprouts, making certain that there is no standing water left in the Easy Sprouter, only wet seeds or sprouts. Be consistent in your rinsing and draining; the sprouts will grow very nicely if you remember to give them their baths. Inconsistent watering habits can cause changes in growth patterns.

The Dual Container System in the Easy Sprouter allows for air circulation, which helps eliminate the chances of mold and mildew growth.

10 Leafy green sprouts are ready to eat in about five to seven days. Start counting the days after the initial soak. Dill and fennel take eight to ten days; garlic and onion can take almost two weeks.

11 Before the harvest, green up the sprouts by exposing them to ordinary daylight for a few hours.

12 Remove the sprouts from the Easy Sprouter and enjoy.

HOW TO SPROUT LEAFY GREENS IN A TRAY SPROUTER

1 Follow safe food-handling procedures by washing the sprouter in warm sudsy water and then rinsing in hot water; use clean water from a reliable source for soaking and sprouting. Wash your hands before touching the seeds or sprouts.

2 Measure your seeds and put them into a jar or bowl of cool water from the tap.

3 Soak the seeds in the jar or bowl overnight, about 8 to 10 hours. You can soak them for up to 24 hours with a water change in the middle at 12 hours.

4 If you want to use fertilizer, add it to the soaking water. You can also put some fertilizer in a spray bottle and mist some on the sprouts as they grow.

5 Pour the seeds into the tray over a sink and let the water drain out. Rinse the seeds in the tray with fresh water and let that water drain. There should be only wet seeds or sprouts in the tray and no standing water. You can use a growing medium for leafy green sprouts. Line the bottom of the tray with the growing medium. You may need to cut it to fit your tray size. The seeds go on top of the growing medium.

6 Some tray sprouters come with solid trays for underneath the tray and lids to cover the tray. Some tray sprouters stack trays on top of each other and the top tray has a cover. These methods are used to create a greenhouse effect so that the seeds and sprouts do not dry out during the sprouting process. Assemble and cover your sprouter according to the manufacturer's guidelines.

7 Approximately every 12 hours, at least two times each day, rinse and drain the seeds or sprouts, making certain that there is no standing water left in the tray, only wet seeds or sprouts. Be consistent in your rinsing and draining; the sprouts will grow very nicely if you remember to give them their baths. Inconsistent watering habits can cause changes in growth patterns. Do not rush; give them some time with the water running over them.

8 Leafy green sprouts are ready to eat in about five to seven days. Start counting the days after the initial soak. Dill and fennel can take eight to ten days; garlic and onion can take almost two weeks.

9 Before the harvest, green up the sprouts by exposing them to ordinary daylight for a few hours.

10 Remove the sprouts from the tray and enjoy.

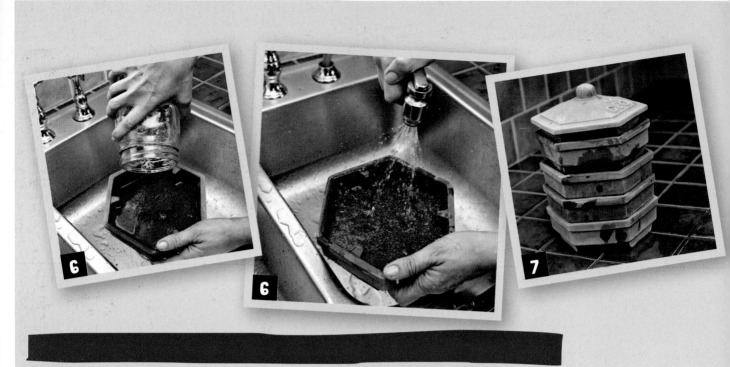

HOW TO SPROUT LEAFY GREENS IN A TERRA-COTTA CLAY SPROUTER

1 Follow safe food-handling procedures by washing the sprouter in warm sudsy water and then rinsing in hot water; use clean water for soaking and sprouting. Wash your hands before touching the seeds or sprouts. Make certain the holes in the tray are cleared and not clogged. You can use a needle or paper clip end to poke out any debris left over from a previous sprouting event.

2 Measure your seeds and put them into a jar or bowl of cool water from the tap.

3 Soak the seeds in the jar or bowl overnight, about 8 to 10 hours. You can soak them for up to 24 hours with a water change in the middle at 12 hours.

4 If you want to use fertilizer, add it to the soaking water. You can also put some fertilizer in a spray bottle and mist some on the sprouts as they grow.

5 Prepare the terra-cotta clay sprouter by presoaking the tray in water for 5 to 15 minutes. The tray will absorb some of the water because it is porous.

6 Remove the tray from the water and pour the soaking seeds into the tray over a sink. Let the water drain out. This may take several minutes because the clay will absorb some of the water. Rinse the seeds in the tray with fresh water and let that water drain. There should be only wet seeds or sprouts in the tray and no standing water.

7 Assemble your sprouter according to the manufacturer's directions.

8 Approximately every 12 hours, at least two times each day, rinse and drain the seeds or sprouts, making certain that there is no standing water left in the tray, only wet seeds or sprouts. Be consistent in your rinsing and draining; the sprouts will grow very nicely if you remember to give them their baths. Inconsistent watering habits can cause changes in growth patterns.

9 Most leafy green sprouts are ready to eat in about five to seven days. Dill and fennel take eight to ten days; garlic and onion can take almost two weeks. Start counting the days after the initial soak.

10 Before the harvest, green up the sprouts by exposing them to ordinary daylight for a few hours.

11 Remove the sprouts from the tray and enjoy.

5

HOW TO SPROUT LEAFY GREENS IN AN EASYGREEN AUTOMATIC SPROUTER

1 Assemble the EasyGreen Automatic Sprouter according to the manufacturer's setup directions. The timer supplied can mist and oxygenate in time increments of approximately 15 minutes.

2 Follow safe food-handling procedures by washing the trays or cartridges in warm sudsy water and then rinsing in hot water; use clean water from a reliable source to fill the water reservoir. Wash your hands before touching the seeds or sprouts. Make certain the holes in the trays or cartridges are cleared and not clogged. You can use a needle or paper clip end to poke out any debris left over from a previous sprouting event.

3 If you want to use fertilizer, add it to the water reservoir.

4 Using an electric automatic sprouter eliminates the need to presoak the seeds. Wet the cartridges with water so that the seeds "stick" and do not jump around from static electricity. Sprinkle an even layer of seeds in a cartridge and shake the cartridge gently from side to side to even out the layer.

5 Put the cartridge in the cavity of the machine. Put in the other empty cartridges as well, so the filled cartridge is on the right side of the cavity and the empty ones are to the left.

Move the seed cartridges daily one cartridge width to the left and place the new seeded cartridges to the far right. This way, you have enough sprouts to eat every day.

6 Leafy green sprouts are ready to eat in about five to seven days. Dill and fennel take eight to ten days; garlic and onion can take almost two weeks. With electric sprouters this time is often shorter because of the more frequent and consistent watering. Replenish the empty cartridges with new seeds to continue the sprouting cycle.

7 Remove the sprouts from the cartridges and enjoy.

THERE ARE A FEW SEEDS THAT FORM A GEL-
LIKE SAC AROUND THE SEED IN THE PRESENCE
OF WATER. THESE SEEDS ARE FLAX, CHIA,
PSYLLIUM, ARUGULA, AND CRESS. MUSTARD CAN
BE SLIGHTLY GELATINOUS, TOO, BUT NOT AS MUCH
AS THE AFOREMENTIONED SEEDS. BECAUSE OF THE
GOOEY SUBSTANCE THEY CANNOT BE SPROUTED
THE USUAL WAY IN JARS OR TRAYS. THEY NEED A
LITTLE BIT OF SPECIAL ATTENTION TO GET PAST
THE GELATINOUS PHASE AND INTO THE ACTUAL
SPROUTING. ONCE YOU KNOW HOW TO GROW THESE
SPROUTS THEY WILL BECOME A REGULAR ADDITION
TO YOUR SPROUTING SCHEDULE.

CHAPTER 7:
GELATINOUS SEEDS

Nutritionally, gelatinous seeds are very close to the leafy green sprouts. Flax, chia, and psyllium are milder tasting sprouts. Arugula sprouts have a very distinct and sharp taste, just like arugula leaves you would put in a salad. Cress is somewhat more peppery in flavor.

Flax is an ancient seed from the Fertile Crescent and the Mediterranean that has been used to produce fibers and can be spun to make linen. Flaxseed oil, or linseed oil, is made by pressing flaxseed. It has a high content of alpha-linolenic acid, which is a form of omega-3 fatty acids and is used as a nutritional supplement. Another way to get the benefits of omega-3s is to grind the seed into flax meal because the seed itself is not digestible in the body. It will pass through the digestive system whole and will swell up in the intestines as it absorbs water, acting like a bulk laxative, sweeping through the intestines. Be sure to drink an extra 8 ounces (235 ml) of water when ingesting flax—either the whole seed or the flax meal—because it absorbs liquid in great quantities. It does not contain gluten.

Chia is an ancient seed cultivated by the Aztecs in pre-Columbian Mexico. It was a food crop that was economically important. The seed itself is very nutritious and easily digested by the body without further processing. One ounce (28 g) of the seed has 9 grams of fat and is a no-cholesterol, gluten-free food. It is a great source of dietary fiber, coming in at 11 grams per ounce (28 g); each ounce also contains 4 grams of protein. It is a good source of calcium, too. Chia seeds, either whole or ground, can be added to smoothies or sprinkled on top of any dish to reap the benefits of this great nutrition. Use them as a substitute for flax, sesame, or poppy seeds in recipes. Mixed in with water or juice it acts like a bulk laxative, sweeping through the intestines.

Psyllium is best known for its use as a bulk laxative, both as a stand-alone supplement and a part of processed breakfast cereals and breads. Arugula and cress are familiar greens in salads. The sprouts add a very different and exciting flavor to any dish.

HOW TO SPROUT GELATINOUS SEEDS

The easiest way to sprout gelatinous seeds is to mix them with other regular sprouting seeds in small quantities. If you are sprouting 4 tablespoons (25 g) of alfalfa or clover, for example, substitute 1 tablespoon (6 g) of chia, arugula, cress, psyllium, or flax. This way, the gelatinous substance is diluted through the other seeds and all will sprout normally.

Gelatinous seeds can be sprouted in jars or trays without any additional efforts when mixed with other regular leafy green seeds. If you wish to sprout the seeds by themselves, then you have three options.

You can sprout them in soil, use a growing medium, or you can use a terra-cotta clay sprouter.

HOW TO SPROUT GELATINOUS SEEDS IN SOIL

Soil absorbs the gooey substance that surrounds the seed when it gets wet and allows the seed to sprout naturally. Use a good-quality potting soil. You do not need much of it because you are growing a sprout, not a fully mature plant. There is no need to soak these seeds before sprouting because they do not behave well when wet.

1 Follow safe food-handling procedures and use clean water from a reliable source; wash your hands before touching the seeds or sprouts.

2 Select a pot or container for your sprouts and fill it with the soil.

3 Sprinkle some dry seed on top of the soil.

4 Keep the soil moist but not soaking wet.

5 If you want to use fertilizer you can put some fertilizer in a spray bottle and mist some on the sprouts as they grow.

6 The seeds will sprout through the soil. After five to seven days they should be ready to harvest.

7 Before the harvest, green up the sprouts by exposing them to ordinary daylight for a few hours.

8 Pick the sprouts from the soil and rinse well. Alternatively, you can cut the sprout above the soil line and rinse well.

You can compost the soil and then reuse it to sprout again.

HOW TO SPROUT GELATINOUS SEEDS IN A TRAY SPROUTER WITH GROWING MEDIUM

It is possible to sprout these seeds in a tray sprouter with a little assistance from a growing medium. Growing mediums are substances that replace soil and can hold many times their weight in water. There are many brands available at some nurseries and specialty stores that cater to growing plants hydroponically, or without soil. You may wish to experiment to find one that you like. The Sure to Grow brand is an easy and effective growing medium that is inert and will not cause mold or mildew to grow.

1 Follow safe food-handling procedures by washing the sprouter in warm sudsy water and then rinsing in hot water; use clean water from a reliable source for soaking and sprouting. Wash your hands before touching the seeds or sprouts.

2 Line the growing medium on the bottom of the tray. You may need to cut it to fit your tray size.

3 Sprinkle dry seed onto the growing medium.

4 Wet the tray with the growing medium and seeds and let the water drain out. There should be only wet seeds and the wet growing medium in the tray and no standing water.

5 If you want to use fertilizer, you can put some fertilizer in a spray bottle and mist some on the sprouts as they grow.

6 Some tray sprouters come with solid trays for underneath the tray and lids to cover the tray. Some tray sprouters stack trays on top of each other and the top tray has a cover. These methods are used to create a greenhouse effect so that the seeds do not dry out during the sprouting process. Assemble and cover your sprouter according to the manufacturer's guidelines.

3

7 Approximately every 12 hours, at least two times each day, rinse and drain the seeds, making certain that there is no standing water left in the tray, only wet seeds or sprouts and the wet growing medium. Be consistent in your rinsing and draining; the sprouts will grow very nicely if you remember to give them their baths. Inconsistent watering habits can cause changes in growth patterns. Do not rush; give them some time with the water running over them.

8 The seeds will sprout through the growing medium. After five to seven days they should be ready to harvest.

9 Before the harvest, green up the sprouts by exposing them to ordinary daylight for a few hours.

10 Cut the sprouts above the growing medium and enjoy.

Most growing mediums cannot be reused.

HOW TO SPROUT GELATINOUS SEEDS IN A TERRA-COTTA CLAY SPROUTER

1 Follow safe food-handling procedures by washing the sprouter in warm sudsy water and then rinsing in hot water; use clean water from a reliable source for sprouting. Wash your hands before touching the seeds or sprouts. Make certain the holes in the tray are cleared and not clogged. You can use a needle or paper clip end to poke out any debris left over from a previous sprouting event.

2 Prepare the terra-cotta clay sprouter by presoaking the tray in water for about 5 minutes, or you can let it sit in water for up to 15 minutes. The tray will absorb some of the water because it is porous.

3 Remove the tray from the water.

4 Sprinkle dry seed onto the terra-cotta tray.

5 Rinse the seeds in the tray with fresh water and let that water drain. This may take several minutes because the clay will absorb some of the water. There should be only wet seeds or sprouts in the tray and no standing water.

6 If you want to use fertilizer you can put some fertilizer in a spray bottle and mist some on the sprouts as they grow.

7 Assemble your sprouter according to the manufacturer's directions.

8 Approximately every 12 hours, at least two times each day, rinse and drain the seeds or sprouts, making certain that there is no standing water left in the tray, only wet seeds or sprouts. Be consistent in your rinsing and draining; the sprouts will grow very nicely if you remember to give them their baths. Inconsistent watering habits can cause changes in growth patterns.

9 After five to seven days they should be ready to harvest.

10 Before the harvest, green up the sprouts by exposing them to ordinary daylight for a few hours.

11 Remove the sprouts from the sprouter and enjoy.

CHAPTER 8:
SHOOTS

BABY BLACK SUNFLOWER OR BLACK OIL SUNFLOWERS, WHOLE BUCKWHEAT, SNOW PEAS FOR SHOOTS, EVEN ADZUKI BEANS AND MUNG BEANS CAN PRODUCE A WONDERFUL LONG, TASTY SHOOT. THESE LARGER SEEDS PRODUCE A LARGER SPROUT, OR SHOOT. THEY TAKE A FEW DAYS LONGER TO REACH MATURITY AND CAN BE USED AS A REPLACEMENT FOR LETTUCE DUE TO THEIR MILD TASTE. BECAUSE OF THEIR HIGH WATER CONTENT, SPROUTED SHOOTS ARE IDEAL FOR JUICING AND ARE BEST GROWN IN A TRAY SPROUTER DUE TO THEIR LENGTH AT MATURITY.

All of these are gluten-free, and the sunflowers, buckwheat, and snow pea shoots can be used as a substitute for wheatgrass juice due to their higher levels of chlorophyll for those who are sensitive to gluten. Even buckwheat, which is not a wheat or a cereal, but is related to sorrel, knotweed, and rhubarb, is gluten-free. In addition to chlorophyll, these shoots are a source of vitamins, fiber, and minerals.

Sprouted shoots are a no-fat, low-sodium, and no-cholesterol food. The carbohydrates they offer are a good source of fiber. This is the good type of carbs, the ones your body needs from unprocessed whole food sources.

HOW TO SPROUT SHOOTS

Shoots are sprouted in either soil or a growing medium. Sunflower, whole buckwheat, and snow peas are typically sprouted in large trays known as standard nursery flats so that you have a volume amount of sprouts at harvest to use. You can also sprout adzuki and mung shoots this way. The trays measure 10 x 20 x 2 inches (25 x 51 x 5 cm). These trays come in two types—with holes and without holes. Put the soil and seeds in the tray with the holes. Then that tray fits inside the solid tray to prevent water and soil from spilling onto kitchen counters or elsewhere in your home. For smaller quantities use a smaller tray—but they are so tasty and versatile, they will disappear quickly, leaving you to wish for more.

It is possible to sprout these seeds in a tray sprouter with a little assistance from a growing medium without using soil. Growing mediums are substances that replace soil and can hold many times their weight in water. There are many brands available at some nurseries and specialty stores that cater to growing plants hydroponically, or without soil. You may wish to experiment to find one that you like. The Sure to Grow brand is an easy and effective growing medium that is inert and will not cause mold or mildew to grow. Shoots grow very nicely in the EasyGreen Automatic Sprouter. Choose the large tray that fits inside the whole cavity to get a volume amount for eating or juicing. Or use the smaller cartridges to get some shoots for each day's consumption.

Sprouted shoots mature somewhere between eight and ten days, shorter in warmer temperatures and longer in cooler temperatures. Before harvesting these sprouts they need to "green up." By exposing them to any ordinary daylight that comes into a room, the process of photosynthesis will begin to develop chlorophyll. It only takes a few hours, for example from breakfast to lunch, to get them green.

GROWING SHOOTS FROM POPCORN

Did you know you can grow shoots from popcorn?

However, not all popcorn will grow into a shoot. The popcorn you purchase at the store for movie night will not sprout; it needs to be fresh popcorn in order to produce shoots. The shoots must be grown in the dark. They need to stay blanched, or white. Grown this way they will stay very sweet and crunchy. These shoots are so sweet they taste like candy. As soon as they green up, the chlorophyll makes them chewy and bitter. Popcorn shoots take about eight to ten days to mature. They are a favorite of top chefs everywhere. Cut the shoot above the corn kernel and enjoy!

HOW TO SPROUT SHOOTS IN A TRAY SPROUTER WITH SOIL

5

6

8

1 Follow safe food-handling procedures and use clean water from a reliable source; wash your hands before touching the seeds or sprouts.

2 Measure the seeds and soak them overnight in a bowl or jar of water. The seeds can be soaked for up to 24 hours with a water change in the middle at 12 hours.

3 If you want to use fertilizer, add it to the soaking water. You can also put some fertilizer in a spray bottle and mist some on the shoots near the roots.

4 After soaking, pour out the water. Rinse with fresh water and pour out the water so that you only have wet seeds.

5 Fill the tray that has holes with soil.

6 Spread the seeds on top of the soil in an even layer.

7 Nestle the tray that has the soil and seeds in it into the solid tray without holes. This will keep any soil and moisture from dripping out.

8 You can cover the tray with a clear humidity dome to help create a greenhouse effect.

9 Keep the soil moist but not soaking wet.

10 The shoots will sprout through the soil. After eight to ten days they should be ready to harvest.

11 Before the harvest, green up the shoots by exposing them to ordinary daylight for a few hours.

12 Cut the shoot above the soil line and rinse well.

You can compost the soil.

HOW TO SPROUT SHOOTS IN A TRAY SPROUTER WITH GROWING MEDIUM

1 Follow safe food-handling procedures by washing the sprouter in warm sudsy water and then rinsing in hot water; use clean water from a reliable source for soaking and sprouting. Wash your hands before touching the seeds or sprouts.

2 Measure the seeds and soak them in a jar or bowl of water overnight. They can soak up to 24 hours with a water change in the middle at 12 hours.

3 If you want to use fertilizer, add it to the soaking water. You can also put some fertilizer in a spray bottle and mist some on the shoots near the roots.

4 Line the growing medium on the bottom of the tray that has the holes. You may need to cut it to fit your tray size.

5 Pour the soaking seeds into the tray.

6 Rinse the seeds with fresh water and let the water drain out. There should be only wet seeds and the wet growing medium in the tray and no standing water.

7 Nestle the tray that has the growing medium and seeds in it into the solid tray without holes. This will keep any soil and moisture from dripping out.

8 You can cover the tray with a clear humidity dome to help create a greenhouse effect.

9 Approximately every 12 hours, at least two times each day, rinse and drain the seeds, making certain that there is no standing water left in the tray, only wet seeds or sprouts and the wet growing medium. Be consistent in your rinsing and draining; the sprouts will grow very nicely if you remember to give them their baths. Inconsistent watering habits can cause changes in growth patterns. Do not rush; give them some time with the water running over them.

10 Shoots are ready to eat in about eight to ten days.

11 Before the harvest, green up the shoots by exposing them to ordinary daylight for a few hours.

12 Cut off the shoots near the root but above the growing medium and rinse well.

HOW TO SPROUT SHOOTS IN AN EASYGREEN AUTOMATIC SPROUTER

1 Assemble the EasyGreen Automatic Sprouter according to the manufacturer's setup directions. The timer supplied can mist and oxygenate in time increments of approximately 15 minutes.

2 Follow safe food-handling procedures by washing the trays or cartridges in warm sudsy water and then rinsing in hot water; use clean water from a reliable source to fill the water reservoir. Wash your hands before touching the seeds or sprouts. Make certain the holes in the trays or cartridges are cleared and not clogged. You can use a needle or paper clip end to poke out any debris left over from a previous sprouting event.

5

3 If you want to use fertilizer, add it to the water reservoir.

4 Using an electric automatic sprouter eliminates the need to presoak the seeds. Wet the tray or cartridges with water so that the seeds "stick" and do not jump around from static electricity. Sprinkle an even layer of seeds in a tray or cartridge and shake the tray or cartridge gently from side to side to even out the layer.

5 Put the tray or cartridge in the cavity of the machine. If you are using cartridges, put in the other empty cartridges as well, so the filled cartridge is on the right side of the cavity and the empty ones are to the left.

Move the seed cartridges daily one cartridge width to the left and place the new seeded cartridges to the far right. This way, you have enough sprouts to eat every day.

6 Shoots are ready to eat in about eight to ten days. With electric sprouters this time is often shorter because of the more frequent and consistent watering. Replenish the empty cartridges with new seeds to continue the sprouting cycle.

7 Remove the shoots from the trays or cartridges, cut off the roots, and enjoy.

CHAPTER 9:
GRASSES

GROWING WHEATGRASS OR BARLEY GRASS AT HOME CAN BE A VERY REWARDING, HEALTHY, AND ECONOMICALLY BENEFICIAL EXPERIENCE. THESE GRASSES ARE FILLED WITH CHLOROPHYLL, THE STUFF THAT MAKES THEM GREEN, AND SHOULD BE JUICED AT MATURITY FOR A WONDERFUL ELIXIR THAT CAN BE TAKEN DAILY OR AT OTHER CHOSEN INTERVALS.

Reactions to the juice differ. Start with a small amount such as a teaspoon (5 ml) and build up to the daily dose of 2 ounces (60 ml) for basic health maintenance taken on an empty stomach, 30 minutes before you drink or eat anything else.

The juice can affect some people who are gluten intolerant, while it does not bother others. You should be careful and watch for symptoms. If you get a reaction to the juice from wheatgrass or barley grass, then change to the gluten-free shoots of sunflower, buckwheat, or snow pea shoots to get your chlorophyll. Alfalfa is another great source of gluten-free chlorophyll. You can use a regular fruit and vegetable juicer and do not need to purchase a special wheatgrass juicer for these shoots. These can also be eaten.

JUICERS

The cellular walls of the blades of grass are difficult for humans to digest. Animals that feed on grass—sheep, goats, cows, and others—are called ruminants. Ruminants have a four-chambered stomach. When you watch these animals eat grass it is swallowed and goes down into the first chamber (rumen). A little later on, they regurgitate that as cud and chew it. Then they swallow that and it goes into the second chamber (reticulum). Sometime later they regurgitate what was in the second stomach, chew it some more, and down it goes into the third part of the stomach (omasum). After it has been there and digested a bit more, it moves to the last part of the stomach (abomasum). That is a lot of digesting!

Because humans do not have a many-chambered stomach and, therefore, cannot properly digest the grasses in the same manner that ruminants can, we juice the grasses to get access to the chlorophyll and other nutrients.

There are two types of wheatgrass juicers available: manual and electric. In either case, the blades of grass are pressed against an auger, which looks like a big screw, and the juice comes out one way and the pulp comes out another way.

The manual juicers are the least expensive of the choices. They do take a little more muscular effort to use than electric juicers and more time, too. But they are handy for when there is no power available and are often a good backup to have if your primary juicer is electric. Choose a manual juicer that is made from stainless steel because it easier to keep clean and is more hygienic.

Electric juicers are more expensive and can be a good investment over time. While they do need access to electricity, they do not take as much effort, and it takes much less time to get the juicing done. Some juicers do both regular fruits and veggies, while others are dedicated to juicing only the grasses. Because the cost of electric wheatgrass juicers can be high, it is wise to do some research to find one that best suits your goals and purpose.

Be careful to choose one that is easy to take apart and clean. Many closets have seldom-used juicers allocated to the top shelf.

If you already own a high-speed blender, it is possible to use it instead of purchasing a juicer. Remember, it is a blender, so you need to start with water; about 1 cup (235 ml) water per $\frac{1}{4}$ cup to $\frac{1}{2}$ cup (57 to 114 g) grass. Then cut the blades of grass into pieces about 1 inch (2.5 cm) or so in length. Put the water in the blender followed by the cut blades of grass. Blend on high for a few seconds. You may get some foam. You can strain the liquid and separate out the solids or let it sit for several minutes and it will separate on its own. This blended juice will be diluted because of the addition of water.

If you find that you do not like the taste of wheatgrass or barley grass juice, then you can mix it with the juices from other veggies. Try to keep to green veggies and do not mix colors or mix it with fruit. When you mix the grass juice with colored vegetables or fruits you dilute the action of the chlorophyll. Try celery, spinach, or kale. You can even use other sprouts such as broccoli, alfalfa, clover, or

MOLD

As the grasses grow, they create their own metabolic heat. Just as you and I have a metabolic heat of 98.6˚F (37˚C) that comes about just because we are living organisms, growing grass creates its own metabolic heat.

Mold is a product of moisture and temperature. To prevent mold from growing you need to lower the temperature of your growing grass. To lower the temperature you can put your growing grass into the refrigerator for several hours each day or overnight. Or you can point a fan directly onto the flats of grass. This will lower the temperature and also increase air circulation, two things that mold does not like. If you are using soil, use a soil that has a pH of 7 or a little bit higher because the grasses enjoy alkaline soil.

Remember not to eat grass that you think may have mold or mildew on it. Discard that grass, sterilize your sprouter, and start over again. It happens to all of us—new sprouters and veterans alike. We all have the capability to grow mold and mildew. Move on to the next batch of sprouts

MANUAL WHEATGRASS JUICER

HOW TO SPROUT GRASSES

Grasses are best sprouted in a tray sprouter due to their length at maturity. If grown in soil or on a growing medium coupled with fertilizer, the juice can be a good source of minerals, amino acids, and some vitamins.

You need to grow a lot of grass to yield a small amount of juice. The grasses are usually grown in large trays known as standard nursery flats. The trays measure 10 x 20 x 2 inches (25 x 51 x 5 cm). These trays come in two types—with holes and without holes. Put the soil or growing medium and seeds in the tray with the holes. Then that tray fits inside the solid tray to prevent water and soil from spilling onto kitchen counters or elsewhere in your home. Grass grown in these trays will yield about 6 to 8 ounces (180 to 235 ml) of juice for 1 ½ to 2 cups (150 to 200 g) of seed.

It is possible to sprout these seeds in a tray sprouter with a little assistance from a growing medium and not use soil. Growing mediums are substances that replace soil and can hold many times their weight in water. There are many brands available at some nurseries and specialty stores that cater to growing plants hydroponically, or without soil. The Sure to Grow brand products are easy to use and inert. You may wish to experiment to find one that you like.

Grasses grow very nicely in the EasyGreen Automatic Sprouter. Choose the large tray that fits inside the whole cavity to get a large amount for juicing.

Before harvesting the grasses they need to "green up." By exposing them to any ordinary daylight that comes into a room, the process of photosynthesis will begin to develop chlorophyll. It only takes a few hours, for example from breakfast to lunch, to get them green.

For wheatgrass, choose hard wheat seeds; for barley grass, choose whole barley. You can also grow other seeds to grass and juice them as well. The nutrition in all of the grasses is about the same, with small differences here and there, and the taste varies a little bit. Try rye or whole oats for grass and do not be afraid to mix them together because their growth and maturation rates are the same.

HOW TO SPROUT GRASSES IN A TRAY SPROUTER WITH SOIL

1 Follow safe food-handling procedures and use clean water from a reliable source; wash your hands before touching the seeds or sprouts.

2 Measure the seeds and soak them overnight in a bowl or jar of water. The seeds can be soaked for up to 24 hours with a water change in the middle at 12 hours.

3 If you want to use fertilizer, add it to the soaking water. You can also put some fertilizer in a spray bottle and mist some on the grass near the roots as it grows.

4 After soaking, pour out the water. Rinse with fresh water and pour out the water so that you only have wet seeds.

5 Fill the tray that has holes with soil.

6 Spread the seeds on top of the soil in an even layer.

7 Nestle the tray that has the soil and seeds in it into the solid tray without holes. This will keep any soil and moisture from dripping out.

8 You can cover the tray with a clear humidity dome to help create a greenhouse effect.

9 Keep the soil moist but not soaking wet.

10 The grass will sprout through the soil. After eight to ten days it should be ready to harvest.

11 Before the harvest, green up the grass by exposing it to ordinary daylight for a few hours.

12 Cut the grass above the soil line, rinse well, and then juice.

13 With this method you can get another growth out of the original planting.

You can compost the soil.

HOW TO SPROUT GRASSES IN A TRAY SPROUTER WITH GROWING MEDIUM

1 Follow safe food-handling procedures by washing the sprouter in warm sudsy water and then rinsing in hot water; use clean water from a reliable source for soaking and sprouting. Wash your hands before touching the seeds or sprouts.

2 Measure the seeds and soak them in a jar or bowl of water overnight. They can soak up to 24 hours with a water change in the middle at 12 hours.

3 If you want to use fertilizer, add it to the soaking water. You can also put some fertilizer in a spray bottle and mist some on the grass near the roots as it grows.

4 Line the growing medium on the bottom of the tray. You may need to cut it to fit your tray size.

5 Pour the soaking seeds into the tray.

6 Rinse the seeds with fresh water and let the water drain out. There should be only wet seeds and the wet growing medium in the tray and no standing water.

7 Nestle the tray that has the soil and seeds in it into the solid tray without holes. This will keep any soil and moisture from dripping out.

8 You can cover the tray with a clear humidity dome to help create a greenhouse effect.

9 Approximately every 12 hours, at least two times each day, rinse and drain the seeds, making certain that there is no standing water left in the tray, only wet seeds or sprouts and the wet growing medium. Be consistent in your rinsing and draining; the grass will grow very nicely if you remember to give it baths. Inconsistent watering habits can cause changes in growth patterns. Do not rush; give the grass some time with the water running over it.

10 Grass is ready to juice in about eight to ten days.

11 Before the harvest, green up the grass by exposing it to ordinary daylight for a few hours.

12 Cut the grass above the growing medium line, rinse well, and then juice.

13 With this method you can get another growth out of the original planting.

HOW TO SPROUT GRASSES IN AN EASYGREEN AUTOMATIC SPROUTER

1 Assemble the EasyGreen Automatic Sprouter according to the manufacturer's setup directions. The timer supplied can mist and oxygenate in time increments of approximately 15 minutes.

2 Follow safe food-handling procedures by washing the trays or cartridges in warm sudsy water and then rinsing in hot water; use clean water from a reliable source to fill the water reservoir. Wash your hands before touching the seeds or grass. Make certain the holes in the trays or cartridges are cleared and not clogged. You can use a needle or paper clip end to poke out any debris left over from a previous sprouting event.

5

3 If you want to use fertilizer, add it to the water reservoir.

4 Using an electric automatic sprouter eliminates the need to presoak the seeds. Wet the tray or cartridges with water so that the seeds "stick" and do not jump around from static electricity. Sprinkle an even layer of seeds in a tray or cartridge and shake the tray or cartridge gently from side to side to even out the layer.

5 Put the tray or cartridge in the cavity of the machine. If you are using cartridges, put in the other empty cartridges as well, so the grass-filled cartridge is on the right side of the cavity and the empty ones are to the left.

Move the seed cartridges daily one cartridge width to the left and place the new seeded cartridges to the far right. This way, you will have enough grass to juice every day.

6 The grass is ready to juice in about eight to ten days. With electric sprouters this time is often shorter because of the more frequent and consistent watering. Replenish the empty cartridges with new seeds to continue the sprouting cycle.

7 Remove the grass from the trays or cartridges and juice it.

GROWING SPROUTS FOR PETS

OUR PET FRIENDS, FURRY, FEATHERY, REPTILES, AND LIZARDS, EAT VEGETABLES. SOME ANIMALS ONLY EAT VEGETABLES AND OTHERS EAT MAINLY GRASS. YOU CAN ENHANCE THEIR FRESH VEGETABLE SOURCE BY SPROUTING FOR THEM.

Sprouts can offer extra fiber to your pet's diet and help keep certain types of chronic diseases like heart disease and diabetes at bay. They have the enzymes needed for strong metabolic functions. Pet immune systems are strengthened by eating fresh sprouts. For farmyard friends, the grasses that you sprout and feed to your pets will be worm-free and can aid in controlling pasture worms and their life cycles, which can be very difficult to eradicate because reinfestation is common.

Cats and dogs can often be seen outside chewing on grass. They like the sweetness the grass offers. Sprouts that are sweet and mild like alfalfa and clover may also be welcomed by your pets. If you have ever purchased cat grass or pet grass from the local market, you know how expensive those small pots of greenery can be. Those grasses

are usually hard wheat, the same seed we use to grow wheatgrass. Sometimes there is a mix of hard wheat, rye, and oats. You only need a few pennies' worth of seed to grow that grass, something that is easily accomplished at home.

There are dog breeders that make their own dog food to ensure the quality of the animals they are raising. Bean and legume sprouts can be found in those home recipes. You can mix some in with your pet's food, store-bought or homemade, to give them a taste of fresh vegetables.

For birds, seeds are a major source of nutrition. Sprouted seeds, just an overnight soak, will be eaten joyfully. Rabbits and other rodent pets like sprouts. Lizards and turtles enjoy fresh veggies as part of their diets, too.

Let's not forget other domesticated animals such as sheep, goats, pigs, and farmyard fowl. Sprouting for them, particularly in the winter months when fresh vegetation may be scarce, will have them come running to you. Fresh sprouted barley grass has made many cows, sheep, and goats very happy.

You may need to experiment with different seeds and different combinations to find what will work for your own pet's needs. Not every pet likes every seed or sprout. You are the one who knows your animals best. Adding fresh sprouts to their daily diets will make them happier and healthier pets.

CHAPTER 10:
WHAT TO DO WITH ALL THOSE SPROUTS

IF ALL OF SUDDEN YOU GET A VERY STRONG
CRAVING TO EAT TACOS, YOU CAN GO TO MANY
DIFFERENT TYPES OF ESTABLISHMENTS AND
PURCHASE TACOS: FAST-FOOD RESTAURANTS,
STREET VENDORS, MEXICAN RESTAURANTS, SOME
DINERS, FROZEN TACOS FROM THE SUPERMARKET,
ETC. HOWEVER, IF YOU HAVE ALL THE
INGREDIENTS AT HOME, YOU CAN MAKE YOUR OWN
TACOS, FRESH, HOMEGROWN, DELICIOUS, AND
CONVENIENT. WHAT COULD BE BETTER?

When you are planning what to make for lunch or dinner, one easy way is to open the refrigerator and pantry, take stock of what is available, and come up with several dishes that go together—pasta and sauce and some veggies, a stir-fry with rice, leftovers from a few days before, a clean-out-the-fridge super salad.

What if you came into the kitchen and decided tonight's meal would include sprouts? Do you have any on hand? Do you have the right type of sprout mature enough to eat? A little planning is necessary in a sprouting kitchen. It takes just a few minutes each week to make certain that you have sprouts ready to eat when needed.

One good way is to start some sprouts each day; this way, you are assured of a continuous supply throughout the week. If you started to soak some leafy green seeds on Sunday, they would be mature enough to eat the following weekend. As soon as they are mature, start soaking more seeds to sprout. If you find that you are finishing your sprouts sooner, then you could start soaking some seeds in the middle of the week in addition to the weekend. Now you have two batches growing and you always have a supply of mature sprouts ready to eat. Beans and grains take only a few days. You could start soaking and sprouting beans every other day. Or soak a large amount of them on Friday and they will be mature enough to eat by Sunday for the week ahead. Change the seeds and beans that you sprout each time to get a variety of different nutrients and flavors.

Another way to plan is to sprout particular seeds for a chosen recipe. Want to make hummus? Then sprout garbanzo beans a few days ahead. Need beans for a stir-fry? Then sprout adzuki and mung. Are you juicing wheatgrass? One standard nursery flat tray yields about 6 to 8 ounces (180 to 235 ml) of juice. Making a raw sprouted soup? Better soak and sprout the sunflowers ahead of time.

Kids love sprouts. They love to watch the seeds grow and change. They love to grab the sprouts right out of the jar or tray and then eat them. They are very curious about taste and texture. Growing sprouts at home can spark children's inquisitive nature and teach them about how plants grow as well as broaden their acceptance of eating vegetables.

Start with mild-tasting sprouts like alfalfa and clover. They are quick to grow and have a wonderful fresh green appearance. Their sweet taste appeals to children. Fenugreek is a nice sprout that has a seed and sprout with an aroma of maple syrup. Mung beans, adzuki beans, and lentils are mild tasting and easily digested. Experiment slowly with the stronger tasting sprouts, especially the ones that add heat, such as radish and mustard. Use these in small amounts mixed in with the milder seeds for older children.

As with all vegetables, eating sprouts decreases the risk of childhood obesity and other chronic diseases. School performance is increased with higher levels of concentration. The vitamins help keep their immune systems functioning and provide the necessary nutrients for growing bodies in good health.

Allowing children to help with the sprouting process—measuring, rinsing, and draining—gives them ownership of the process and keeps them involved. What you teach them early in life is what will stay with them for years to come.

Introducing sprouting to your children will give them a lifelong source of cholesterol-free and low-calorie food for snacks and meals. Sprouts are a great source of enzymes that help our bodies carry out metabolic functions like digestion. Increasing daily fiber intake will help them have healthy colons. Vitamins, minerals, protein, and good carbs are all found in sprouts. This is a habit that, started in childhood, will stay with them throughout their lives.

Many children prefer to eat sprouts right out of the tray or jar. But they can also be juiced, or put into a smoothie. A handful of sprouts in a fruit-based smoothie or one with yogurt will not change the taste or color of the smoothie but will give a nutritional boost. Sprouts go great with other raw veggies like carrots, peppers, celery, and tomatoes. You can arrange them on a plate for little fingers to grab. Put some lentil sprouts in the next bowl of soup just before eating to get some crunchy sweet goodness.

If you are following a recipe, do not be afraid to substitute one sprout for another. Does the recipe call for alfalfa? You can use clover or fenugreek. Does the recipe need adzuki? Try mung or even green pea. Buckwheat greens substitute nicely for sunflower greens, as do snow pea shoots. Quinoa can fill in for millet. You can experiment and note what changes you made. Who knows? The recipe may turn out better than planned.

Your rate of consumption determines how and when to start seeds to sprout. Soak and sprout some seeds each day so that you always have fresh sprouts ready to eat to satisfy any craving that comes about or to prepare a recipe.

SERVING SUGGESTIONS FOR SPROUTS

Some of us are purists when it comes to eating sprouts. We eat them directly out of the sprouting container or tray. There is no need to cover the wonderfully fresh taste of the new vegetables with toppings, dressings, or seasonings. Each sprout has its own flavor and texture. No further processing necessary. But not everyone wants to eat just the sprout, and even purists need a change now and then. Raw sprouts can be eaten in a variety of ways with a little bit of further preparation. These methods will give you ideas for how to eat sprouts so that you can add them to your daily diet. Eat some sprouts every day and try to eat them at every meal to add fiber, vitamins, and minerals to your diet.

COLD LEAFY SOUP WITH ITALIAN SEASONING

SOUPS

Raw sprouted soups can use up a variety of mature sprouts that you have around, or you can plan ahead and sprout seeds specifically for the soup. Mix and match what you use to have some mild flavors and some hotter flavors. These soups are very cooling on hot summer days and keep in the fridge for a few days.

COLD LEAFY SOUP

This soup works great on its own, or it can be dressed up with any of the seasoning combinations below for a tasty and healthy meal. Mix up the flavors—use some mild ones like alfalfa, clover, or fenugreek; use some greens like sunflower, buckwheat, or snow pea shoots; add a small amount of heat like radish or mustard; and garnish with onion or garlic sprouts.

3 ½ cups (175 g) chopped sprouts

1 to 2 cups (235 to 470 ml) water

1 cup (150 g) diced carrot, tomato, or celery or fresh peas

Seasoning combination of choice (recipes follow)

This raw sprouted soup needs no heating or cooking. Just assemble the ingredients and enjoy!

Yield: 2 servings

ITALIAN SOUP SEASONING

Basil

Marjoram

Oregano

Rosemary

Thyme

Serve with a good crusty loaf of Italian bread and olive oil for dipping.

MIDDLE EASTERN SOUP SEASONING

Ground cumin

Ground coriander

Salt

Cayenne pepper

Serve with sprouted garbanzo bean hummus and pita bread wedges.

MEXICAN SOUP SEASONING

Chili powder

Salt

Cumin

Garlic powder

Oregano

Onion powder

Paprika

Serve with taco chips and salsa.

ORIENTAL SOUP SEASONING

Tamari

Powdered ginger

Garlic powder

Onion powder

Prepared mustard, hot or sweet

Serve with crunchy noodles.

COLD LEAFY SOUP WITH ORIENTAL SEASONING

COLD BEAN OR LENTIL SOUP

This is another delicious raw soup, and a great way to use your bean or lentil sprouts. Try it with any of the seasoning ideas on page 135.

....

3 ½ cups (175 g) variety of bean or lentil sprouts

Chopped vegetables of your choice

1 to 2 cups (235 to 470 ml) water

....

This raw sprouted soup needs no heating or cooking. Just assemble the ingredients and enjoy!

....

Yield: 2 servings

COLD BEAN OR LENTIL SOUP

HOT BEAN OR LENTIL SOUP

HOT BEAN OR LENTIL SOUP

When beans are added to hot water they do
not lose nutrition or enzymes the way they
do when cooked for a long time over heat.
Warmed up this way, beans may be easier to
digest for some people. Miso is a fermented
paste of soybeans, sometimes with rice
or barley added. Miso can be found in the
refrigerated section of health foods stores.
Use darker miso for colder temperatures and
light miso for warmer weather.

1 tablespoon (16 g) miso

1 cup (235 ml) hot water, almost but not yet
boiling

¼ to ½ cup (25 to 50 g) sprouted beans or
lentils

Dissolve the miso in the hot water. Add the
sprouted beans or lentils.

Yield: 1 serving

SALADS

Sprouts can be put on top of any lettuce-based or chopped vegetable salad. You can also make a salad of just sprouts.

Before you make the salad, think of a simple dressing to use. You may have a bottled dressing that you enjoy, but you can also make your own. A simple vinaigrette works—olive oil, red wine vinegar, and salt. Use balsamic vinegar for a different flavor. Substitute lemon juice for a fresh, tart taste. You can also just eat the sprouts without any dressing and enjoy the flavors on their own.

Try using some pickled vegetables as a topping to your salads—chopped pickled beets or pickled radish perks up sprout salads. An olive tapenade or even sauerkraut makes for an interesting change of pace.

LEAFY SPROUTED SALAD

LEAFY SPROUTED SALAD

¹⁄₂ cup (25 g) alfalfa sprouts

¹⁄₂ cup (25 g) clover sprouts

¹⁄₂ cup (25 g) radish or mustard sprouts

¹⁄₂ cup (25 g) broccoli or kale sprouts

Combine all the ingredients in a bowl and top with your favorite dressing.

Yield: 2 servings

QUINOA SALAD

SALAD OF SHOOTS

½ cup (25 g) chopped sunflower greens

½ cup (25 g) chopped buckwheat greens

½ cup (25 g) chopped snow pea greens

½ cup (50 g) adzuki shoots

½ cup (25 g) mung bean shoots

Popcorn shoots, for garnish

Combine all the ingredients in a bowl and top with your favorite dressing.

Yield: 2 servings

QUINOA SALAD

If available, a mix of black, red, and traditional white quinoa makes a visually impressive salad.

1 cup (50 g) sprouted quinoa

Combine all the ingredients in a bowl. A vinaigrette of olive oil, vinegar, and salt complements the quinoa. A little bit of finely chopped orange or apricot is a nice addition.

Yield: 2 servings

LENTIL SALAD

BEANS AND GRAINS SALAD

With beans and grains together, you get a wide assortment of essential proteins, the ones our bodies cannot manufacture on their own.

....

¼ cup (25 g) sprouted lentils

....

¼ cup (13 g) sprouted hard wheat, soft wheat, or rye

....

Combine all the ingredients in a bowl and top with your favorite dressing.

....

Yield: 1 serving

BEAN SPROUT SALAD

¼ cup (13 g) Mung Bean Sprouts

¼ cup (13 g) Adzuki Bean Sprouts

¼ cup (13 g) French Lentil Sprouts

¼ cup (13 g) Green Pea Sprouts

¼ cup (13 g) Leafy sprout like alfalfa, clover or cabbage

Combine all the ingredients in a bowl and top with your favorite dressing.

Yield: 2 servings

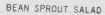

BEAN SPROUT SALAD

SANDWICHES AND WRAPS

Now you can travel with your sprouts for work or play. Take them on a picnic and use the mature sprouts you have available with old favorites like peanut butter or burgers. A few radish or mustard sprouts add an extra kick.

DELI DELIGHTS

DELI DELIGHTS

Take two pieces of your favorite bread or a wrap, add some protein—turkey, chicken, ham, cheese—put some sprouts on top of that, add mustard or mayonnaise, and now you have a great sandwich. For liverwurst use some onion sprouts and strong mustard. Don't forget the dill pickle!

PEANUT BUTTER AND SPROUTS

PEANUT BUTTER AND SPROUTS
Take your favorite bread or wrap, spread it with peanut butter, sprinkle with chile pepper or Thai pepper, and add mild leafy green sprouts like alfalfa, clover, or sunflower greens to offset the chile pepper. A really delicious combination!

BURGERS AND SPROUTS
Instead of lettuce and tomato on the burger bun, use some sprouted sunflower greens or snow pea shoots. The larger greens will stand up to the strong meat flavors.

BURGERS AND SPROUTS

BEAN SPROUT SPREAD

BEAN SPROUT SPREAD

Take some sprouted beans and run them through a food processor or food grinder; you may need to add a little oil or water because bean sprouts do not hold a lot of moisture. Spread on bread and top with leafy sprouted greens.

RAW SPROUTED HUMMUS

Hummus is great when spread on bread or used in wraps. Top with leafy sprouts for added deliciousness.

2 cups (200 g) sprouted garbanzo beans (sprout 1 cup [200 g] dried garbanzo to yield about 2 cups [200 g] sprouted garbanzo)

3 to 5 tablespoons (45 to 75 ml) lemon juice, to taste

2 tablespoons (30 g) tahini (sesame seed paste)

2 cloves garlic, crushed

½ teaspoon salt

2 tablespoons (30 ml) olive oil

Combine all the ingredients in a food processor until it becomes a paste. Add water a little bit at a time if needed.

Yield: 8 servings

RAW SPROUTED HUMMUS

JUICING SPROUTS

The process of juicing separates the fiber from the vegetable or sprout. When you use a juicer, you get juice out of the spout and what is left is the pulp.

Wheatgrass and barley grass need a special juicer (see page 118), but for the other leafy sprouts you can juice them using a regular fruit and vegetable juicer. The best sprouts to juice are the leafy greens and the shoots. Bean sprouts and lentils do not juice well because they do not have a lot of moisture in them. Adding a bunch of sprouts to any juice, even fresh fruit juice, will not alter its appearance or flavor, but will add a great deal of nutrition.

Juicing sprouts is a great way to use an overload of mature sprouts. You can juice just the sprouts or juice them in combination with other vegetables. Adding a little bit of radish, mustard, onion, or garlic sprouts to the juice gives it a bit of kick.

A fusion of great tastes awaits! Try these combinations:

1 Sunflower sprouts, clover sprouts, radish sprouts, carrot

2 Buckwheat, celery, garlic, or clover sprouts

3 Fenugreek sprouts, alfalfa sprouts, mustard sprouts, cucumber

4 Kale sprouts, raw or sprouted onion, clover sprouts, mature kale

5 Cabbage sprouts, clover sprouts, carrot

BLENDING SPROUTS

When you use a blender you use everything the sprout has to offer, including the fiber. Before blending sprouts, add some water to the container first, and then add the sprouts. Blending breaks up the fibers of vegetables on the cellular level. Sprouts that have been blended are easier to digest because of this. It is a good way to get nutrition to those who are having difficulty eating.

Try these combinations:

1 Radish sprouts, clover sprouts, tomato, avocado

2 Green pea sprouts, alfalfa sprouts, carrot, ginger root

3 Fruit (apple, pear, or peach) and a handful of alfalfa or clover. The little bit of sprouts will not change the flavor or texture of the blended fruit but will offer more great nutrition.

4 Kale sprouts, radish sprouts, cucumber

5 Sunflower sprouts, radish sprouts, clover sprouts, celery

DEHYDRATING SPROUTS

The process of dehydrating removes water from a sprout as a means of preservation. It also makes them crunchy. You can purchase a dehydrator to get the job done, or use your oven. The dehydrator will be more efficient than the oven because the trays let air flow over and under the sprouts, but you can start with your oven to find out whether you like the dehydrated result. With dehydrating you can make crunchy seasoned snacks that will be favorites at parties and get-togethers. Some nutrition will be lost through the dehydration process, but not much, and it helps to have a variety of ways to eat more sprouts.

Grains can be soaked, sprouted, and then dehydrated, which makes them a crunchy alternative for a breakfast cereal in the morning. They can also be ground into flour for further processing.

Beans and lentils can be sprouted and seasoned before dehydrating to make a great crunchy snack that will keep you away from potato chips.

To dehydrate sprouts, use the lowest setting possible on your oven. Place sprouts in an even layer on a cookie sheet. You may want to use parchment paper so they do not stick to the cookie sheet. During the time in the oven, stir the sprouts to obtain even drying. This can take a while—anywhere between 4 and 8 hours or more. Dehydrated sprouts are ready when they are crispy and crunchy. Taste for doneness.

SNACKING SPROUTS

While sitting in front of the computer or in your favorite chair watching television, try reaching for sprouts as a snack instead of chips, pretzels, or candy. Just plain, right-out-of-the-sprouter sprouts. Sprouted marrowfat peas are crunchy, mild, and sweet, the candy of the sprouting world. They need no dressing or preparation to be enjoyed. There is nothing like grabbing a handful of leafy green sprouts from a tray while working on the computer, and when the work is over and the tray of sprouts is finished, you feel energized and refreshed, ready to move on to the next task—a different sort of feeling from the fullness and sluggishness you can get from eating processed snacks.

EASY GUIDE TO SPROUTING

To get the best results while sprouting, follow the guidelines in this chart. Some general tips that apply to all sprouts are as follows:

1. Measurements are not scientific; your yield may differ.
2. Sprouts take longer to mature in cooler temperatures, less in warmer temperatures.
3. Germination takes place above 65°F (18.3°C).
4. Store seeds at 60°F (15.6°C) or below; a refrigerator or freezer is fine.
5. Store mature sprouts in an airtight container in the refrigertor for about one week. Rinse and drain periodically so sprouts do not dry out.

	DRY MEASURE	YIELD	SOAKING INSTRUCTIONS	LENGTH OF SOAKING
BREAKFAST GRAINS				
Buckwheat groats	½ cup (100 g)	¾ cup (120 g)	Jar or bowl of water	8 to 10 hours; overnight; can be soaked for 24 hours with a water change in the middle at 12 hours
Hulless oats	½ cup (40 g)	1 cup (100 g)	"	
Hulled barley	½ cup (100 g)	¾ cup (120 g)	"	
SMALL GRAINS				
Amaranth	½ cup (85 g)	¾ cup (140 g)	Do not soak	Not applicable
Millet	½ cup (85 g)	¾ cup (140 g)	Jar or bowl of water	2 to 4 hours
Quinoa	½ cup (85 g)	¾ cup (140 g)	"	"
SMALL LEAFY GREEN SEEDS				
Alfalfa	¼ cup (25 g)	8 cups (400 g)	Jar or bowl of water	8 to 10 hours; overnight; can be soaked for 24 hours with a water change in the middle at 12 hours
Broccoli	"	"		
Cabbage	"	"	"	
Clover	"	"	"	
Fenugreek	"	"	"	"
Mustard	"	"	"	"
Radish	"	"	"	"
Kale	"	"	"	"
Dill	"	"	"	"
Fennel	"	"	"	"
Onion	"	"	"	"
Garlic	"	"	"	"
SHOOTS				
Sunflower for greens with black shells	1 pound (454 g)	2 pounds (908 g)	Jar or bowl of water	8 to 10 hours; overnight; can be soaked for 24 hours with a water change in the middle at 12 hours
Whole buckwheat for greens	"	"	"	
Snow pea shoots	"	"	"	"
Popcorn	"	"	"	"
BEANS AND LEGUME SEEDS				
Green peas	1 cup (100 g)	1 ½ to 2 cups (75 to 100 g)	Jar or bowl of water	8 to 10 hours; overnight; can be soaked for 24 hours with a water change in the middle at 12 hours
Marrowfat peas	"			
Lentils	"	"	"	
Mung	"	"	"	
Adzuki	"	"	"	"
Garbanzo	"	"	"	"
Soy	"	"	"	"

BEST TOOL FOR SPROUTING	TIME TO SPROUT	RINSING INSTRUCTIONS	NEED TO GREEN UP?	NOTES
Jar or bowl used for soaking	8 to 10 hours; overnight	Just before eating; drain well	No	Use these for a morning breakfast cereal and for pie shell crusts and other recipes.
"	"	"	"	
Jar or bowl	1 to 3 days	Two times each day; drain so there is no standing water	No	These seeds are very tiny and do not need a long soak or they may explode. You may or may not see a sprout but they are okay to eat even if you do not.
"	1 to 2 days		"	
"	"		"	
Jar, Easy Sprouter, tray sprouters, terra-cotta clay sprouter, EasyGreen Automatic Tray Sprouter	5 to 7 days	Two times each day; drain so there is no standing water	Yes	Although small these seeds offer a powerhouse of nutrition and taste, they only need a few hours to become green.
"	"	"	"	
"	"	"	"	
"	"	"	"	
"	"	"	"	
"	"	"	"	
"	8 to 10 days	"	"	
"	"	"	"	
"	10 to 14 days	"	"	
"	"	"	"	
Tray sprouters, terra-cotta clay sprouter, EasyGreen Automatic Tray Sprouter, standard nursery flats	8 to 10 days	Two times each day; drain so there is no standing water	Yes	The sprouts from these seeds grow tall and do better in tray sprouters. They green up in a matter of hours and can be used as a substitute for organic lettuce. These can also be grown in moist soil.
"	"		"	
"	"	"	No	Popcorn shoots need to be grown in the dark to stay sweet.
Jar, Easy Sprouter, tray sprouters, terra-cotta clay sprouter, EasyGreen Automatic Tray Sprouter	1 to 2 days	Two times each day; drain so there is no standing water	No	The quickness of these sprouts makes them easy to have every day.
"	"	"	"	
"	"	"	"	
"	"	"	"	
"	"	"	"	

	DRY MEASURE	YIELD	SOAKING INSTRUCTIONS	LENGTH OF SOAKING
GRASS SEEDS				
Whole barley for grass	2 cups (200 g)	6 to 8 ounces (180 to 235 ml) juice	Jar or bowl of water	8 to 10 hours; overnight; can be soaked for 24 hours with a water change in the middle at 12 hours
Hard wheat	"	"	"	
Whole oats for grass	"	"	"	
GELATINOUS SEEDS				
Arugula	¼ cup (25 g)	8 cups (400 g)	No soaking	Not applicable
Cress	"	"	"	"
Flax	"	"	"	"
Chia	"	"	"	"
Psyllium	"	"	"	"
EDIBLE SEEDS				
Pumpkin	½ cup (75 g)	½ cup (75 g)	Jar/bowl of water	4 to 6 hours
Hulled sunflowers	½ cup (75 g)	1 cup (150 g)	"	"
Unhulled sesame	½ cup (75 g)	1 cup (150 g)	"	"
Hulled sesame	½ cup (75 g)	½ cup (75 g)	"	"
SPROUTED WHOLE GRAINS				
Rice	½ cup (90 g)	1 cup (180 g)	Jar or bowl of water	8 to 10 hours; overnight; can be soaked for 24 hours with a water change in the middle at 12 hours
Rye	"	"		
Hard wheat	"	"	"	
Soft wheat	"	"	"	
Triticale	"	"	"	"

BEST TOOL FOR SPROUTING	TIME TO SPROUT	RINSING INSTRUCTIONS	NEED TO GREEN UP?	NOTES
Standard nursery flat, tray sprouter, terracotta clay sprouter, EasyGreen Automatic Sprouter " "	8 to 10 days " "	Two times each day; drain so there is no standing water "	Yes " "	A large amount of grass yields a small amount of juice. The chlorophyll in the juice is healthful. These can also be grown in moist soil.
A pot with soil, terra-cotta clay sprouter, tray sprouter with growing medium " "	5 to 7 days " " " "	Keep soil moist; rinse terra-cotta clay sprouter and sprouter with growing medium two times each day and drain so there is no standing water	Yes " " "	Once you handle the gooey stuff, these seeds sprout just like alfalfa.
Jar or bowl used for soaking " "	1 to 2 days " "	Just before eating; drain well " "	No " "	These edible seeds add a nice level of protein and crunch to any dish.
Jar, Easy Sprouter, tray sprouters, terra-cotta clay sprouter, EasyGreen Automatic Sprouter " "	1 to 2 days " " " "	Two times each day; drain so there is no standing water " " "	No " " " "	Sprouted grains add a sweet taste and chewy dimension to salads and stir-fries.

RESOURCES

USEFUL WEBSITES

AMAZON
www.amazon.com
Search for "The Sprout House"

MUMM'S SPROUTING SEEDS (LOCATED IN CANADA)
www.sprouting.com

NUTRITION DATA
http://nutritiondata.self.com

THE SPROUT HOUSE
www.sprouthouse.com
Organic sprouting seeds, organic sprouting seed mixes, organic wheatgrass and organic barley grass seeds and supplies, Easy Sprout sprouter, hemp sprouting bag, sprout master trays, Geo Sprouter, Geo terra-cotta clay sprouter, Miracle Exclusives terra-cotta sprouter, EasyGreen Automatic Sprouter, stainless steel screens, plastic lids, fertilizers, growing medium, standard nursery flats, clear humidity domes for wheatgrass and barley grass.

SPROUT PEOPLE
www.sproutpeople.org

U.S. FOOD AND DRUG ADMINISTRATION
www.fda.gov

BOOKS

Braunstein, Mark
The Sprout Garden
www.markbraunstein.org

Meyerowitz, Steve
Sprouts, The Miracle Food
www.sproutman.com

Meyerowitz, Steve
Wheatgrass: Nature's Finest Medicine

Simonsohnm, Barbara
Barley Grass Juice

Wigmore, Ann, and Lee Pattinson
The Blending Book

SPROUTERS AND OTHER PRODUCTS

EASYGREEN AUTOMATIC SPROUTER
www.easygreen.com

EASY SPROUTER
www.sproutamo.com

GROWING MEDIUM
www.suretogrow.com

HEMP SPROUTING BAG
www.sprouthouse.com

SPROUT AND GRASS FERTILIZERS
www.neptunesharvest.com

SPROUT MASTER TRAYS
www.lifesprouts.com

TERRA-COTTA CLAY SPROUTER AND JUICERS
www.miracleexclusives.com

VITAMIX
www.vitamix.com

ACKNOWLEDGMENTS

Writers working alone at the keyboard to keep the cursor dancing across the blank white screen with words do not work in a vacuum. My family joyfully supported and encouraged me throughout this project. Thank you to my husband, Paul, for being as excited as I am. To Matthew, my son, for your words of enthusiastic encouragement. Also to my parents for their love and enjoyment of the whole process; and to my brothers, John and Mark, and their families. I know how happy you have been for me and with me.

I would like to thank Tiffany Hill of Quarry Books for contacting me and asking if I would like to write a book about sprouting. Little did she know that she would help me fulfill one of my lifelong dreams: to become a published author. And to Renae Haines for continuing the editing process and supplying her great and creative marketing ideas.

I am thankful for my art director, Regina Grenier, whose attention to detail brought out the scrumptiousness of sprouts. She worked tirelessly to set up the shots, meticulously adding items to build scenes right from Tuscany. Abbondanza!

I had a whole team assigned to this project from Quarry Books, some of whom I never had contact with but who worked to bring this book alive. Thanks to all of you.

I am grateful for the splendid photos from Thea Conklin. Each of the shots is a wonderful, beautiful, masterful piece of art. She was able to show how much I love the allure of the seeds and the sprouts through her camera lens.

A big note of thanks to Mark Braunstein for reading my manuscript and helping me to get all the details correct. He paved the way by sharing his knowledge and time so freely.

Many thanks and much love go to my very good friends Susan and Bernie Bolitzer, for allowing us the use of their home for the photo shoot.

The DAM Cafe and Deli in Saugerties, New York, provided us with great food, beautifully presented, during the intense three-day photo shoot.

Much gratitude goes to the Writers' Club at the Saugerties Public Library for the opportunity to write with friends. Abundant thanks to my great friend Frank Finley, the real writer, for his encouragement and prodding to keep writing throughout the years. I never felt alone because you have all been with me.

Most of all, I would like to thank all of my clients. This book is born out of the questions that you have asked me over the years. These words and paragraphs, coupled with the photos, are my answers gathered together in one place for you. Now, it is time to get out the seeds and start to soak them. Let the sprouting begin!

ABOUT THE AUTHOR

Rita Galchus, popularly known as "Sprout Lady Rita", is the owner of The Sprout House. She started sprouting in April 1986 after attending a free class about sprouting with her husband while they were dating. That class started her love of sprouting. She purchased the business in October 2000 and has been Sprout Lady Rita ever since. Rita holds bachelor's degrees in business management and holistic nutrition.

Through The Sprout House, she sells tons of organic sprouting seeds every year and instructs people in how to sprout. In addition to her love of sprouting, she is an avid reader and also enjoys walking, sewing, crafts, beach vacations, and spending time with her family and friends. She lives with her husband and son.

INDEX